Llewellyn's

Witches' Datebook

2013

Featuring

Art by Jennifer Hewitson
Text by Elizabeth Barrette, Raven Digitalis,
Dallas Jennifer Cobb, Ellen Dugan,
Ember Grant, James Kambos, Melanie Marquis,
Susan Pesznecker, and Tess Whitehurst

ISBN 978-0-7387-1518-6

2013

JANUARY
S	M	T	W	T	F	S
		1	2	3	4	5
6	7	8	9	10	11	12
13	14	15	16	17	18	19
20	21	22	23	24	25	26
27	28	29	30	31		

FEBRUARY
S	M	T	W	T	F	S
					1	2
3	4	5	6	7	8	9
10	11	12	13	14	15	16
17	18	19	20	21	22	23
24	25	26	27	28		

MARCH
S	M	T	W	T	F	S
					1	2
3	4	5	6	7	8	9
10	11	12	13	14	15	16
17	18	19	20	21	22	23
24	25	26	27	28	29	30
31						

APRIL
S	M	T	W	T	F	S
	1	2	3	4	5	6
7	8	9	10	11	12	13
14	15	16	17	18	19	20
21	22	23	24	25	26	27
28	29	30				

MAY
S	M	T	W	T	F	S
			1	2	3	4
5	6	7	8	9	10	11
12	13	14	15	16	17	18
19	20	21	22	23	24	25
26	27	28	29	30	31	

JUNE
S	M	T	W	T	F	S
						1
2	3	4	5	6	7	8
9	10	11	12	13	14	15
16	17	18	19	20	21	22
23	24	25	26	27	28	29
30						

JULY
S	M	T	W	T	F	S
	1	2	3	4	5	6
7	8	9	10	11	12	13
14	15	16	17	18	19	20
21	22	23	24	25	26	27
28	29	30	31			

AUGUST
S	M	T	W	T	F	S
				1	2	3
4	5	6	7	8	9	10
11	12	13	14	15	16	17
18	19	20	21	22	23	24
25	26	27	28	29	30	31

SEPTEMBER
S	M	T	W	T	F	S
1	2	3	4	5	6	7
8	9	10	11	12	13	14
15	16	17	18	19	20	21
22	23	24	25	26	27	28
29	30					

OCTOBER
S	M	T	W	T	F	S
		1	2	3	4	5
6	7	8	9	10	11	12
13	14	15	16	17	18	19
20	21	22	23	24	25	26
27	28	29	30	31		

NOVEMBER
S	M	T	W	T	F	S
					1	2
3	4	5	6	7	8	9
10	11	12	13	14	15	16
17	18	19	20	21	22	23
24	25	26	27	28	29	30

DECEMBER
S	M	T	W	T	F	S
1	2	3	4	5	6	7
8	9	10	11	12	13	14
15	16	17	18	19	20	21
22	23	24	25	26	27	28
29	30	31				

2014

JANUARY
S	M	T	W	T	F	S
			1	2	3	4
5	6	7	8	9	10	11
12	13	14	15	16	17	18
19	20	21	22	23	24	25
26	27	28	29	30	31	

FEBRUARY
S	M	T	W	T	F	S
						1
2	3	4	5	6	7	8
9	10	11	12	13	14	15
16	17	18	19	20	21	22
23	24	25	26	27	28	

MARCH
S	M	T	W	T	F	S
						1
2	3	4	5	6	7	8
9	10	11	12	13	14	15
16	17	18	19	20	21	22
23	24	25	26	27	28	29
30	31					

APRIL
S	M	T	W	T	F	S
		1	2	3	4	5
6	7	8	9	10	11	12
13	14	15	16	17	18	19
20	21	22	23	24	25	26
27	28	29	30			

MAY
S	M	T	W	T	F	S
				1	2	3
4	5	6	7	8	9	10
11	12	13	14	15	16	17
18	19	20	21	22	23	24
25	26	27	28	29	30	31

JUNE
S	M	T	W	T	F	S
1	2	3	4	5	6	7
8	9	10	11	12	13	14
15	16	17	18	19	20	21
22	23	24	25	26	27	28
29	30					

JULY
S	M	T	W	T	F	S
		1	2	3	4	5
6	7	8	9	10	11	12
13	14	15	16	17	18	19
20	21	22	23	24	25	26
27	28	29	30	31		

AUGUST
S	M	T	W	T	F	S
					1	2
3	4	5	6	7	8	9
10	11	12	13	14	15	16
17	18	19	20	21	22	23
24	25	26	27	28	29	30
31						

SEPTEMBER
S	M	T	W	T	F	S
	1	2	3	4	5	6
7	8	9	10	11	12	13
14	15	16	17	18	19	20
21	22	23	24	25	26	27
28	29	30				

OCTOBER
S	M	T	W	T	F	S
			1	2	3	4
5	6	7	8	9	10	11
12	13	14	15	16	17	18
19	20	21	22	23	24	25
26	27	28	29	30	31	

NOVEMBER
S	M	T	W	T	F	S
						1
2	3	4	5	6	7	8
9	10	11	12	13	14	15
16	17	18	19	20	21	22
23	24	25	26	27	28	29
30						

DECEMBER
S	M	T	W	T	F	S
	1	2	3	4	5	6
7	8	9	10	11	12	13
14	15	16	17	18	19	20
21	22	23	24	25	26	27
28	29	30	31			

Llewellyn's Witches' Datebook 2013 © 2012 by Llewellyn Worldwide, 2143 Wooddale Dr., Dept. 978-0-7387-1518-6, Woodbury, MN 55125-2989.

Editing/design by Ed Day

Cover illustration and interior art © 2012 by Jennifer Hewitson

Art on chapter openings © 2006 by Jennifer Hewitson

Table of Contents

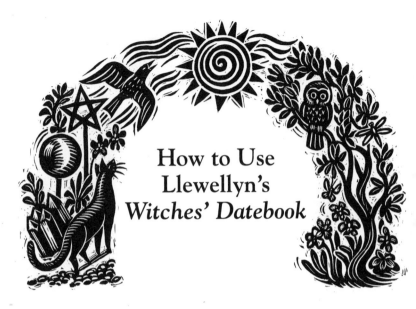

How to Use Llewellyn's Witches' Datebook

Welcome to *Llewellyn's Witches' Datebook 2013*! This datebook was designed especially for Witches, Pagans, and magical people. Use it to plan sabbat celebrations, magic, Full Moon rites, and even dentist and doctor appointments. At right is a symbol key to some of the features of this datebook.

MOON QUARTERS: The Moon's cycle is divided into four quarters, which are noted in the calendar pages along with their exact times. When the Moon changes quarter, both quarters are listed, as well as the time of the change. In addition, a symbol for the new quarter is placed where the numeral for the date usually appears.

MOON IN THE SIGNS: Approximately every two and a half days, the Moon moves from one zodiac sign to the next. The sign that the Moon is in at the beginning of the day (midnight Eastern Time) is noted next to the quarter listing. If the Moon changes signs that day, there will be a notation saying "☽ enters" followed by the symbol for the sign it is entering.

MOON VOID-OF-COURSE: Just before the Moon enters a new sign, it will make one final aspect (angular relationship) to another planet. Between that last aspect and the entrance of the Moon into the next sign it is said to be void-of-course. Activities begun when the Moon is void-of-course rarely come to fruition, or they turn out very differently than planned.

4

PLANETARY MOVEMENT: When a planet or asteroid moves from one sign into another, this change (called an *ingress*) is noted on the calendar pages with the exact time. The Moon and Sun are considered planets in this case. The planets (except for the Sun and Moon) can also appear to move backward as seen from the Earth. This is called a *planetary retrograde*, and is noted on the calendar pages with the symbol ℞. When the planet begins to move forward, or direct, again, it is marked D, and the time is also noted.

PLANTING AND HARVESTING DAYS: The best days for planting and harvesting are noted on the calendar pages with a seedling icon (planting) and a basket icon (harvesting).

TIME ZONE CHANGES: The times and dates of all astrological phenomena in this datebook are based on Eastern time. If you live outside the Eastern time zone, you will need to make the following changes: Pacific Time subtract three hours; Mountain Time subtract two hours; Central Time subtract one hour; Alaska subtract four hours; and Hawaii subtract five hours. All data is adjusted for Daylight Saving Time.

Planets

☉ Sun	♆ Neptune
☽ Moon	♇ Pluto
☿ Mercury	⚷ Chiron
♀ Venus	⚳ Ceres
♂ Mars	⚴ Pallas
♃ Jupiter	⚵ Juno
♄ Saturn	⚶ Vesta
♅ Uranus	

Signs

♈ Aries	♐ Sagittarius
♉ Taurus	♑ Capricorn
♊ Gemini	♒ Aquarius
♋ Cancer	♓ Pisces
♌ Leo	
♍ Virgo	**Motion**
♎ Libra	℞ Retrograde
♏ Scorpio	D Direct

1st Quarter/New Moon ☽   3rd Quarter/Full Moon ☺
2nd Quarter ☽   4th Quarter ☽

○ **Tuesday** ← Day and date
1st ♎ ← Moon's quarter and sign
2nd Quarter 4:01 am ← Moon quarter change   Planting day → 🌱
☽ v/c 4:01 am ← Moon void-of-course
☽ enters ♏ 9:30 am ← Moon sign change/ingress
♄ ℞ 10:14 am ← Planetary retrograde   Harvesting day → 🧺
Color: Gray ← Planetary retrograde
← Color of the day

5

Magick on a Rainy Day
by Melanie Marquis

Like the plants of the earth, through the rain, we thrive. A rainy day presents a great opportunity to connect with nature and work fast-acting, life-enhancing magick. Rain is both a part of nature's cycle and a direct reflection thereof; heated by the sun, liquid water on the earth's surface turns to vapor and rises up to the sky, where it transforms into a liquid once more before returning to the earth to repeat the process. In a single raindrop are held the energies of death and rebirth, manifestation and dissipation, destruction and creation. Rain is the essence of water, the power of the sky, the sacrifice and sustenance of the earth. Through practicing rainy-day magick, we improve our ability to create positive changes in our lives that are harmonious with the balance and cycle of the natural world. Our understanding of nature increases, and we gain new magickal skills to expand our repertoire. The next time raindrops fall on your head, don't be glum—open an umbrella and your magickal mind, and take it as a chance to try something new! Here are some ideas to get you started.

Rain Gods and Goddesses

Since ancient times, many deities have been called on to bring rain, calm storms, and enhance the fertility and fruitfulness of the earth. In Rome, Jupiter (aka Jove), was king of the gods and king of the rains; one of his names was Jupiter Pluvius, "bringer of rain." In Greece, his equivalent was Zeus, god of thunder, rain, and lightning. In southern

Africa, the Zulu people honored Mbaba Mwana Waresa, goddess of rain and rainbows. Tlaloc, the rain god in Aztec society, was the consort of the goddess Chalchiuht-licue, who ruled over all the earth's waters. In Maori legend, Ua was a powerful rain god who had several names highlighting his various aspects—Ua-Roa meaning "long rain," Uanui meaning "great rain," and Ua Nganga meaning "rain-

storm." In Aboriginal mythology, Bunbulama was the goddess of rain.

If you would like to work with rain gods and goddesses, you might place a cup of water on your altar and draw raindrops, lightning bolts, or other appropriate symbols on your body or around your ritual space. Call the deity by name. If you sense a divine presence, introduce yourself respectfully, then listen quietly with an open heart and mind for guidance and insights. Once you're on friendly terms, you can ask the deity or deities for help in your magickal workings for rain, fertility, creativity, purification, and other water-themed spellwork. Thank the rain deities with living plants or offerings of pure, fresh water.

Raindrop Meditations

Listening to the rain fall can be a very relaxing and mystical experience; utilize the next rainy day as a catalyst for deep meditation that will benefit you magickally. Try this. Sit indoors quietly and comfortably, letting the sounds of rain hitting the roof fill your mind and spirit. Envision yourself, your soul, as the earth, and sense the rain falling into you, strengthening and nourishing the body of the world that is reflected in your earthly form. Let the sound of the rain soothe you and enjoy a feeling of closeness and unity with nature and its gifts.

For an outdoor rainy-day meditation, look around until you find a body of water or a large puddle. Watch the raindrops hit the surface of the water, and notice the concentric, outward flowing ripples created by the impact. Think about how our every action, our every feeling and every thought, has its effects on the energies surrounding us. Find your center, your core being, and envision how you would like the love and joy within you to impact the world around you, just as a single drop of rain casts circles of energy into the surrounding water.

Cleansing Rain Charms

Next time the forecast calls for rain, try this simple charm to rid yourself of worries or other misfortunes. Soon after it starts to sprinkle, take a piece of chalk outside and write on concrete or a large rock a word or sentence expressing what you wish to let go. Think about your desire for liberation from your woes. As the rain washes away the chalk, so too will your grievances be washed away. Another way to experience the cleansing benefits of rain is to simply be in it; take a walk or stand outside and let the drops hit your body and wash away stale energies. You'll feel infused with the refreshing powers of earth, water, and sky.

Rain Potions

Rain is an excellent base for many potions. As rain may contain pollutants, it's best to keep these blends for external use only. Rain potions can be dabbed on the body, used to anoint or wash magickal tools, sprinkled in ritual spaces, homes, and other locations—the possibilities are as boundless as your imagination!

Bottle rain in an earthen jug for a ready-made potion perfect for boosting creativity. For a potion to enhance feelings of love, set out a clear glass container during a gentle rain and collect the drops. Add a piece of rose quartz or a few rose petals to magnify the potion's power. Save rain from a thunderstorm for a powerful potion to bring about major changes or transformations. Collect it in an opaque, preferably black container, and mark the jar or bottle with a lightning bolt.

If you see rain falling while the sun is shining brightly, place a blue bottle outside and you'll soon have a potion that is great for bringing happiness and soothing anxieties. This potion is also ideal for manifesting good luck. Anoint your wallet, the soles of your feet, and the front door of your house for maximum benefit.

Save nighttime rain for a psychic-boosting power potion; for best results, seal it up in a silver container. When you are using a divination tool such as tarot, runes, or a scrying mirror, place thirteen drops of the potion around the area where you are doing the reading to increase your ability to receive and interpret psychic visions.

Mud Magick

Get in touch with nature and connect with powerful earth energies by getting down and dirty with some rainy-day mud magick. If you have a need for some banishing magick, try this spell. Wait for the rain to saturate the dirt, then scoop up the mud in a bowl, adding more rain or soil to suit until you have a thick, clay-like mixture that feels just right. Shape the mud into  a flattened disk about the size of your palm. Use a toothpick or slender twig to mark the disk with a glyph symbolizing what you wish to banish. If banishing grief, you might draw a frowning face on the mud token. To banish a dangerous foe, mark the disk with the person's initials. Now place the disk on the ground and let the rain pour upon it. Call on the energies of the sky and the rain to help along the spell, and watch as the rain erodes the mud disk, banishing the energies symbolized therein.

Umbrella Spells

Umbrellas make excellent tools for rainy-day magick. Associated with sky gods, rain can carry your wishes to the powers that be, and it tends to do so rather swiftly. Try this bit of attraction magick and get ready for quick, positive results. Draw a symbol of your wish on the outside, convex part of an umbrella. Take a walk in the rain, twirling the umbrella clockwise as you envision what you want. If more love is what you're after, draw a heart on the umbrella and imagine your life filled with passion, caring, and romance as the rain spins off the twirling umbrella.

Likewise, if there is something you wish to diminish, simply draw an appropriate symbol on an umbrella and envision your magickal goal as you spin the umbrella counterclockwise in the falling rain.

Let It Pour!

From umbrella spells to powerful potions, mystical meditations to rituals for transformation, rain presents many opportunities for personal and magickal growth. Potent, swift, and practical, rain can be an ideal medium for spellwork, and through experimentation and imagination, the scope of your rain magick will expand by leaps and bounds. Let the falling rain soothe your soul, open your heart, and inspire your mind; a rainy day is a chance to tune in and listen as nature has her say.

Putting Yourself Out There

by Raven Digitalis

That wretched broom closet! How many Witches are in there these days? Quite a few, though I would imagine that the number has significantly decreased since I first started studying occultism. While it's amazing to see so many practitioners out in full flight on their proverbial broomsticks, the general public still knows very little about us.

I certainly consider myself an advocate of what may be the next step in the process: spreading public awareness. If you're comfortably out of the broom closet, there are numerous ways you can work on increasing public understanding of our paths.

Personal or Public Platforms

I used to proudly display my pentacle necklaces and talismans on a daily basis, but now I only wear jewelry on occasion. Some practitioners find it advantageous to wear sacred jewelry both for self-protection and to help educate people who might inquire about the meaning of the symbolism. This sort of pride-and-activism-through-education approach is a great first step in getting acquainted with the variety of views the general public has toward Pagan and magickal paths.

If you feel comfortable with public speaking, consider speaking at public rallies or as a Pagan representative for university panels (chat up the Anthropology and Sociology departments—they love us!), or by hosting workshops and lectures in your local community. If you're skilled at writing, taking a few minutes to compose letters to the editor of local and international magazines and newspapers can go a long way—in fact, media outlets tend to count one person's feedback as "one voice of many" in terms of their readership or viewership. In other words, your letter can help shape a media outlet's approach to the topic. This, in turn, has a ripple effect on a vast number of readers or viewers. Your chosen media feedback doesn't have to be anything grandiose or even mention your spiritual path. I've found that post-cards are extremely effective in reaching large media outlets, as they are easy to read, while short e-mails (that can be easily copied and pasted) are more apt to make it into print. Personally, I utilize both methods simultaneously on a regular basis.

Adapt to the Audience

There's nothing wrong with not referring to yourself as "Witch" if you're not fully devoted to the cause, or feels the term limiting for whatever reason. One of the most beautiful things of twenty-first century spirituality is that we all have the option of both researching and blending varying cultures and their practices. While I definitely consider myself a Witch, for example, I am also a Thelemite, a magician, an occultist, an empath, a moderate psychic, a tarot reader, and a shaman of sorts. My foundation, however, is Wicca and Neopagan Witchcraft, which is why I enjoy bringing public attention to that particular sphere. Both media outlets and the public at large respond to different titles and labels differently, which is why it's important to make adjustments depending on the situation. If I'm communicating with the media, I have no problem with slightly altering my vocabulary and the terms with which I refer to myself to accommodate a news outlet. If I were to write a letter to the editor to a Christian magazine, I may refer to myself as a mystic and healer instead of a Pagan or a Witch, simply because the tailored approach is likely to reach a greater audience, thus getting my views and opinions across *without* being untrue to myself or lying.

While you may wear a more New Age hat for one media outlet, or a nature-worshipper's hat for another, Samhain is the ideal time for donning your Witch hat. Newspapers, magazines, local media, and international media sources love to delve into the Halloween mythos at this time. Why not bask in the glory of our typical Hallow's stereotypes? It's the perfect opportunity to dispel common myths.

While many practitioners shy away from the terms "faith," "belief," or "God," these terms are easily digestible by the public at large who are comfortable with these common terms. You risk unnecessary scrutiny by publicly discussing your Gnostic experience of connecting with elemental nature spirits, but a discussion about your belief in the interconnectedness of humanity and nature may get more favorable feedback.

Without question, the mere stereotype of the word "Witch" can turn off some folks. Discussing some of the similarities between Craft and Native American spirituality or Wicca's roots in Masonry and old Celtic harvest cycles can instead give people a more positive and realistic view from the get-go. Just the same, many people aren't ready to drop their prejudices and won't listen to a thing you say, but don't worry: that's their problem, not ours.

A Focus on the Common Cause

If you're serious about putting yourself out there, remember that you will be seen as a representative for our community—even if you repeatedly say that you are not the voice for all Witches (or what-have-you). It's unavoidable. For this reason, it would be foolish to approach public situations with anger or hostility unless a severe violation of human or animal rights is occurring. It would be unmindful to bash other religious or political groups—even if you're speaking out against their intolerance. It would be silly to profess a greater understanding of the universe than other people who really may be trying their best. When dealing with the public, you are a voice for our community, like it or not. While this may evoke an intimidating sense of responsibility, it dually blesses you with a cosmic freeze-frame high-five for your bravery in spreading awareness at the cost of judgment.

When dealing with the media or the public at large, it's wise to emphasize the importance of diversity. By honing your focus on the more easily digestible and loving sides of the spectrum, we reach a much larger audience. By discussing your views about human compassion and acceptance, you give a positive name to ethical occultists, aiding in the evolution of religious expression and global unity.

Along those lines, if you feel drawn to civil rights, poverty, or another cause, you can show others what you stand for by getting involved in your community and helping other marginalized members of society. There are many, but one group that is often overlooked is prisoners. Prison Ministry work involves helping inmates learn their rights, practice their ceremonies, and head in a healthy direction. Very often, those who genuinely regret past behaviors are in the greatest need of healing, support, and friendship.

You must also know your history. Many less-tolerant religious groups quite frankly rely on hearsay as historical fact—we don't want to fall into that category. Don't shy away from academic literature; it's quite often one of our greatest resources for understanding spiritual and religious evolution. Many historical theories change over time as new findings are revealed. A significant example is the period of the witch hunts. For years, many practitioners professed the idea of nine million Witches burnt on the stake by the Roman Catholic Church in the Middle Ages. More accurately, however, academics have settled on a figure of about 40,000 to 50,000 *accused* Witches (who are loosely, if at all, connected to modern witchcraft) mostly killed by *hanging* in the early modern times. Additionally, Wicca is a modern fusion practice based in Masonry, Celtic Paganism, the Western Grimoire traditions, and other systems—*not* some ancient persecuted-but-preserved goddess cult. By rigorously researching our history, we can present a more educated and realistic evolution of our community to those who are curious to learn more.

Because our lifestyle is absolutely not one of converting others to our relatively dogma-free practices, I believe it's our right and responsibility to open the magickal door for people who might be interested. Putting yourself out there, in the public sphere, is one way we can help spread awareness of our history and practices, and give a great number of individuals an expanded view of their spiritual options. The simpler the approach and the greater the community backing, the more accessible and acceptable our important messages become to the public.

As a final word, remember that we Pagans, Wiccans, magicians, occultists, shamans, mystics, and so on, are *all fruits of the same tree.* Though more and more practitioners are keen to distance themselves from labels they may not fully identify with, it's essential to remember our magickal and spiritual unity—and stick together as a likeminded community—when spreading public awareness of our uncommon ways.

Cauldron Magic and Lore

by James Kambos

My personal interest in cauldrons began on a winter afternoon many years ago. My grandfather called to say that my Uncle Elton had died. Uncle Elton was a gentle man, who had a passion for going to estate sales and farm auctions near his home in rural northern Ohio. My parents and I were asked to go through the treasures he'd collected over the years—a massive undertaking—and to take whatever we wanted. Among the old bottles, tools, and kitchen gadgets, there was one item that caught my eye. It appeared to be a rusty old cooking pot. It had a handle, straight sides, a curved bottom, and three legs. Why it intrigued me, I'll never know, but there it was: my first cauldron!

At the time, I had no idea that this old-fashioned pot was actually a cauldron or that it was associated with magical traditions deeply rooted in antiquity. It did, however, spark my imagination. I could picture it hanging over a country hearth on a cold snowy day, while a farm wife simmered a hearty soup or stew in it.

After returning home with my rare find, I painted it black. Over the years, it served as a container for pots of flowers, or in the fall I filled it with pumpkins and gourds. It was much later that I learned it was a cauldron and that it was a symbol of the Craft. Soon I began to realize its mystical significance, and its deep connection to the magical wisdom of long lost ancient civilizations.

A Rich Magical Tradition

Cauldrons, along with the broom, pointed hat, and black cat, have been a symbol of witchcraft for centuries. The theater, television, and movies have played a part in helping with this association. Shakespeare's *Macbeth*, television's *Bewitched*, and of course, Harry Potter, have all helped to remind the public of the cauldron's connection with witchcraft well into the twenty-first century. While this isn't a bad thing, it should be understood, however, that cauldrons have been a potent magical tool since before recorded history. And, of all magical tools, the cauldron is probably the only one that has helped advance civilization.

That may sound odd, but think about it. Before the cauldron, primitive societies depended on heavy earthenware pots to prepare food. To do this, stones had to be heated in a fire then added to the cooking liquid to heat it. When the cauldron came about, the cooking process greatly improved. Cauldrons were portable and could be placed directly over a fire. As a result, food became more nutritious and was prepared more quickly.

It's no surprise that the cauldron went from being a humble cooking pot to become a valuable magical tool. In time, it became highly regarded as an instrument of spiritual and physical transformation, as well as renewal. First and foremost, it utilized all four of the natural elements. Fire was used to heat it, water was used to fill it, herbs or vegetables represented earth, and the steam/aromas which arose out of it, represents the element, air. Out of the cauldron came food, healing balms, medicines, teas, magical potions, or just water for cleansing.

Due to its shape, and because women usually tended it, the cauldron became especially associated with feminine magic and the female mysteries. It symbolized the Goddess, the womb, birth, death, rebirth, and all creation. The three legs found on most cauldrons remind us of the three aspects of the Goddess—Maiden, Mother, and Crone. The legs can also symbolize the three lunar phases—waxing, full, and waning.

When a cauldron is stirred however, with a spoon, stick, or a ceremonial knife, this introduced the God aspect. This being the case, when any of these implements is placed inside a cauldron the female and male forces are symbolically united, bringing about some form of creation.

Throughout history, many diverse civilizations have regarded the cauldron as having magical powers. It was seen as a source for bounty, health, inspiration, wisdom, and regeneration. The concept of "The Cauldron of Regeneration," a belief that the cauldron is a vessel of death as well as rebirth, was widely held. This belief is associated with the Celtic goddess Cerridwen, and the Babylonian goddess Siris. The Greek goddess Medea used her cauldron to restore youth. In many instances, sacrificial cauldrons appear in Celtic and Norse mythology.

The cauldron is mainly linked with the Goddess, however certain gods are also associated with cauldron magic. The Celtic horned god, Cernunnos, for example, is depicted on the richly decorated silver Gundestrup cauldron discovered in Denmark in 1891. This cauldron, which was discovered in a Danish peat bog, dates back to 100 BCE. It may have been placed there by Druids as an offering to their deities. The Norse god Odin was to have obtained special powers by drinking magic blood from a cauldron.

But the most dramatic tale about a god and his cauldron focuses on the giant Welsh cauldron god, Bran. One of his symbols was the cauldron, and he used it to resurrect slain warriors. Interestingly, he was finally killed in battle by a poison arrow, but only after his magic cauldron had been destroyed. Bran's Cauldron of Rebirth is believed to be the basis for the Christian legend of the Holy Grail.

Cauldron Spells

A cauldron can be used as a holder for a candle, an incense burner, or as a decoration. But, its role as a tool for magical transformation makes it an ideal aid for spell work. Keep in mind however, salt is corrosive to cast iron, so if you need to use salt for a spell ingredient, don't leave it in your cauldron for long periods.

If you wish to use a cauldron to enhance your magic, here are a few spells and magical techniques to get you started.

Scrying: A cauldron is a perfect scrying aid. You could simply fill the cauldron half-full with water, relax, and begin to scry. But, here are some other methods.

To scry during a Full Moon, place a silver coin, quartz crystal, or moonstone in the bottom of a cauldron. Fill half full with water, light a silver candle, and scry. If possible, do this outside or near a window.

Here is a wax or oil method. After filling with water, light a new white candle and hold it above the cauldron. Let some of the hot wax drip into the water. As the drops solidify, "read" their shapes. The wax technique was frequently used to answer love questions. Another method is to dribble a few drops of olive oil on the water. Focus on the oil droplets to receive a message. This is an old Mediterranean form of scrying.

A Banishing Spell: This spell will rid you of a bad habit or problem, or stop gossip. For this spell you'll need to wear a simple ceremonial robe, or even a shawl. Place an empty cauldron in the middle of your altar. On either side, light two white candles for banishing, or two gray candles to stop gossip. In a gesture of gratitude, raise the cauldron, then place it back on the altar—upside down. Now, let your robe fall to the floor, symbolizing you're free of your problem. Lastly say:

This problem (or gossip) is passing harmlessly out of my life, back into the void, in the best possible way. So mote it be.

Snuff out the candles.

A New Image Spell: Light a red candle; place it in front of your cauldron. Take a photo of yourself, showing whatever it is you don't like—hair, weight, etc. Ignite this in the candle's flame, let it burn in the cauldron. Then cut a photo of the way you'd like to look out of a magazine, or sketch your new image yourself. Put this picture in front of the red candle. Say this charm:

The old me is vanishing harmlessly without a trace. A perfect new me is taking its place. So mote it be.

A Protection Spell: To avert any evil or psychic attack aimed at you, try this. At night, fill your cauldron with water and add a pinch of dried wormwood. Leave the cauldron just inside your front door. Stir the water three times in a counterclockwise direction with the blade of a ceremonial knife and say:

Cauldron black, and trusty knife; banish any evil which may be sent to harm my life.

Leave the knife in the cauldron overnight. In the morning, cleanse the blade and pour the water out, away from your home.

Cauldrons still inspire us. Trophies given as prizes for sporting events and to athletes are an echo of the magic cauldrons given as gifts to the warriors of ancient times. The America's Cup yacht race is a perfect example.

And every four years, millions of people worldwide are inspired by the most famous cauldron of all—the Olympic Cauldron, which along with the Olympic Flame, presides over the Olympic Games.

Thousands of years have passed since a simple cooking pot called a cauldron first appeared over a long-forgotten campfire. But time has not diminished our fascination with this ancient symbol of the Craft.

Staying Positive

by Tess Whitehurst

We might define each of our individual lives as "a complex interweaving of feelings that makes up our everyday experience." Our job as magical practitioners is to become conscious of the subtleties of this interweaving: to work with it and shape it according to our will and desires. And, because we all dwell in the same sea of energy, when we harmonize our own energies, everyone else—and the entire universe—benefits.

That's all well and good while we're sitting at home meditating in front of our altar or standing in a grove of trees drawing down the Moon. But what about when we're in the dentist's waiting room (when we have a paralyzing fear of the dentist)? Or what about when we're in a rush and we can't seem to find a parking space? Or what about when we feel forced to deal with that coworker who always appears to be out to get us?

I'll tell you what: employ a little magical first aid and put those tricky situations to work for you.

First: Say "Yes"

In just a moment, we'll go into some practical ways to shift the tide and make those tricky situations work for you. But for now, please note that the first rule of business with magical first aid is to say a resounding "Yes!" to the situation rather than being in denial about it or trying to fight it. "Wait! But don't we want to *change* the situation?" you may

be thinking. Yes. But everything is simply a feeling, so what we really want to change is *our relationship with it*. Then, everything else will follow. So first, we must behave as if (and truly believe) that it is exactly what is supposed to be happening for our truest good and most ideal spiritual unfolding.

"But why?" you may be thinking. Because once we fully accept and even love the situation as it is, we are already changing it. We are becoming one with it. We are entering the stream so that we can move with it rather than against it, which means that we can benefit from the power it holds, and be clear and focused as we make choices about what to do next.

As difficult as it might seem difficult to say an inner "yes" to a nasty coworker or something that terrifies you, I assure you that it's easier than saying an inner "no." Just rest assured that saying "yes" to something does not mean that you have to live with it! Quite the opposite, in fact: it's the fastest way to begin to reduce the power that it holds over you.

So to clarify, saying "yes" to the moment does not mean saying "Yes, it's okay that this person is treating me unkindly," or whatever—it's saying "*Yes*, this person is treating me unkindly, and *Yes*, I don't like it very much, and *yes*, I know that somewhere in this situation there is a hidden blessing, and *yes*, I accept this challenge fully."

Preventative (Energy) Medicine

Okay, now let's go back a few steps and see if we can stop at least a few unpleasant situations before they even start. For sensitive people like us, energetic clearing and shielding are absolute musts. It's also imperative that we practice daily intention setting and what might be called "programming our day."

All of this can be done very simply and succinctly in the morning before you leave the house. For example, you might sit comfortably, with your spine straight and eyes closed, and perform the following meditation:

Relax and take some deep breaths. Then continue to watch your breath as it naturally goes in and out until you notice it becoming deeper on its own. Consciously relax your body. Now call on a helper of your choice (I like to call Archangel Michael) to help clear and vacuum your entire body and energy field of all undesirable/congested energies and energetic cords of fear. Then, ask the helper to

shield you and encompass you in a sphere of very bright white light and then very bright indigo/violet light "in which only love remains, through which only love may enter." As you reside in this sphere, visualize and inwardly affirm the things you'd like to experience in this day. See everything unfolding in a beautiful way, and feel the feelings that go along with pleasant surprises and lucky breaks. Also take some time to visualize spheres of protection around your home, car, and loved ones, and call on any divine helpers you wish.

On-the-Spot Protection

Even when we've done our morning work (as above), we can sometimes encounter situations that are notorious fear triggers, such as walking down a dark alley or driving home in a snowstorm. In situations like this when we feel our physical well-being may be threatened, while of course we must take every precaution possible and appropriate in the physical realm, we can also work in the energetic realm to protect ourselves and bring about feelings of comfort and calm.

In the dark alley, for example, you might ask for angelic protection and feel that you have very tall, imposing body guards of light walking in front of you, behind you, and to both sides of you.

Or, in the snowstorm, you might say a quick invocation, such as "St. Christopher, thank you for surrounding my car in a bubble of protective light and for helping me arrive home safe and sound."

Other on-the-spot protections include visualizing a mirrored sphere around your body and aura, mentally bathing yourself in the intoned sound "Om," and connecting deeply with the molten power at the core of the earth.

Divine Life Support

Another way to move out of fear or discord is to immediately elevate yourself spiritually out of the conflict or situation and into the realm of the divine. I learned this one when I first began my work as a feng shui consultant. Anytime I was in someone's house and I began to feel unsure or overwhelmed, I consciously rose above my ego and merged my consciousness with the divine consciousness (which is, of course, all there is in truth). This is not easy to explain, but it's easy to do. Instead of thinking about how to do it, just feel your way into it and imagine pulling yourself upwards out of the illusion of conflict or fear and into the infinite consciousness of the God and Goddess, where all wisdom resides.

Transmutation Therapy

Here's another angle. Anger, fear, and discord generate a lot of energy. Why not transmute that negative energy into positive energy and make it work for you? One way to do this is to call on Saint Germain (he's not a Catholic saint, he's an ascended alchemical master who just happened to have the word "Saint" in his last name). I ask him to infuse the situation with his signature violet light, which immediately transmutes negativity into positivity and blessings. Or, you can mentally surround yourself with a giant lotus blossom and empower it with the intention to transform negativity into beauty and freshness in the same way a lotus blossom draws its pristine beauty from out of the muddy depths. When transmuting, be sure to breathe deeply!

Luck Transfusions

Then there are those times when we feel that we need a miracle, or a lucky break, or even just a parking spot! During times like these, take a

moment to notice what your inner dialogue is. If it's, "Oh no, I can't find a spot, I can't find a spot," or "Not again! Why can't I get what I want just this one time?" you're just not putting your magical abilities to work for you. Instead, how about conjuring up the feeling that you already have exactly the item or break or miracle that you're wishing for? Breathe into the feeling and feel gratitude that it is already a part of your life experience. You might even say "Thank you so much Goddess for my perfect parking spot!" or "Thank you so much for my beautiful new apartment! I love it so much!"

Healthy Habits

To stay in the flow of positivity and positive life conditions, and to keep your spirits high, I suggest incorporating these three healthy habits into your day.

First and foremost, drink at least half your body weight in ounces per day! This will help keep your energy clean and clear and help you cleanse both physical and energetic toxins out of your system. You might also like to add flower or gem essences to help fine-tune your outlook and mood.

Second, eat a good amount of fresh (ideally organic) fruits and vegetables to nourish your energy field with color and vibrant life energy.

Third, whenever possible, get a good night's sleep and rejuvenate your mind, body, spirit, energetic boundaries, and magical power.

Strength Training

When you think about it, challenges are the things that make us stronger, wiser, and more magically powerful. So go forth, heal yourself, heal others, stay positive, and enjoy the adventure that you call your life!

Moon
Void-of-Course
by Dallas Jennifer Cobb

Moon void-of-course is a fascinating time astrologically speaking, but one we hear and read very little about. Considering its profound effect on our lives, we need to know more about it in order to harness its energy to work with us and for us, instead of against our every effort.

Understanding what moon void-of-course is, how it influences our lives, and what activities are best avoided or undertaken during this period will save you time, energy, money, and worry.

Lunar Influence

We know that the Moon, because of its proximity to earth, has enormous effect on people, plants, water and energy. Among other things, it strongly influences emotion, intuition, fertility, and growth. The Moon travels around the earth about every twenty-nine days. As it passes through each astrological sign, the Moon embodies different influences and energy as influenced by the personality of the sign it's visiting. The phases of the Moon also have distinct influences and effects.

Besides the phases of the Moon or its position within the astrological signs that influences energy, but also the relationships the moon forms with other planets, and of course, when it is "void-of-course."

What is Moon VOC?

While the Moon makes its rounds traveling from one astrological sign to another in its orbit, it forms major aspects, or relationships, to other planets. When the Moon is not in relationship—when its not forming a conjunction, sextile, square, opposition, or trine with any planet—it's said to be in an "aspect vacuum," commonly referred to as "moon void-of-course."

Moon void-of-course happens about thirteen times in each lunar cycle, occuring every couple of days. Because our calendar months can be anywhere from twenty-eight to thirty-one days long, it is possible for fewer or more void-of-course periods to occur within one month. The void-of-course period can last for a moment, or up to almost two and a half days. On calendars that note lunar influences, Moon void-of-course is notated as Moon VOC, or just V/C.

VOC Influences

Because the Moon has such profound effect on all living creatures, people, animals and even plants are affected by the void-of-course energy. If we think of "void-of-course" as meaning without direction, or in a vacuum of influence, then consider that the effect on us is similar. We can be directionless, unfocused, and foolhardy when the Moon is void-of-course. Consider what daily activities can be affected by this energy.

Decision-making suffers from "directionless" tendencies, so we can become muddled, confused, and wishy-washy. Motivation is disrupted, so our completion of tasks, follow-through, and efficiency is adversely affected. Communication can become less direct, with messages getting lost, screwed up, or misunderstood. And often, as a result of these influences or because of the direct effect of the "aspect vacuum" the Moon is experiencing, our relationships flounder.

Psychologically speaking, during a Moon void-of-course period, many people feel spacey, detached, and somehow "out of it." That lack of lunar energy coming in can leave us feeling empty, lacking, and even tired; and without our usual relationships which help to define us, we can feel lost, alone, and uncertain psychologically.

What to Avoid

Wondering what you should avoid during a Moon void-of-course period? Many astrologers agree that avoiding most activities is a good idea, especially things for which you desire a specific, straightforward, outcome. Consider what might be affected by unfocused and directionless energy, and a tendency toward poor decision-making and judgment.

It's best not to buy anything, plan something in detail, make decisions or commitments, or undertake large purchases, because matters entered into when the Moon is void-of-course are unlikely to come to real fruition or progress smoothly along a predictable path.

Consider the effect of Moon void-of-course on a new relationship of either a business or personal nature. Because anything started during the void-of-course period don't usually last, try to avoid first dates, starting a business, and even job interviews. Remember, the energy at the time suggests "no relationships," and a vacuum or void.

Sound judgment is affected by the void-of-course influence, so do not consult a professional seeking medical diagnosis, legal judgment or opinion, or even diagnosis of machines or engines. Avoid making significant new purchases, major life decisions, or entering into binding contracts or agreements. The directionless influences increase the chance of buying things you neither want nor need, making choices that lead nowhere, and entering into agreements which may never be honored. Last but not least, try to avoid assembling, counting, or sharing things, because it could result in people becoming very aware of your mistakes, shortages, or errors.

The tendency toward interrupted communication suggests that you should avoid any crucial, important discussions in this time. Your words can become distorted or misunderstood, telephone messages can get lost or garbled, fax machines are more likely to malfunction, orders can be shipped incomplete, and even e-mail can be lost in the digital ether.

And with a total void of incoming lunar energy it is best to avoid magical work during the void-of-course period. Without a supply of lunar energy to fuel your magical work, you might end up drawing upon your own energy for fuel, and this could leave you feeling even more depleted.

What to Do during VOC

Without outside influence or stimulation, it is as if we, too, are in stasis when the Moon is void-of-course. The pause button has been pushed, and momentarily little is required of us. So, plan to "do" little. Just be.

During Moon void-of-course, many of us turn within to the quiet self, looking for our own interpretation, ideas, and answers. Without lunar influence, position, or aspect, it is an ideal time to focus on our own inner work, the quiet spiritual work needed to stay clear, centered, and magically attuned. Prayer, meditation, and contemplation are excellent activities to undertake during Moon VOC, as are journaling, reflection, and contemplation. While praying or meditating, we are free of the pull of lunar influences and other planetary relationships, so better able to connect with our higher selves, intuition, and deepest spirit. Moon void-of-course can allow us to hear that  quiet inner voice that gets crowded out when we are busy "doing."

Many people find mind-body exercises like yoga or Pilates useful in facilitating a calm, inner focus while staying active in the outside world or on the physical plane. Turned in, we commune with ourselves and our bodies, the relationships that too often get neglected in favor of our daily interactions.

Use this time to relax, let go of expectations, sleep, laze on the couch, and be free of the continual push and pull energy of daily, mundane living. Enjoy the benefits of rest, relaxation, and quiet time. Read, reflect, or catch up on the maintenance tasks of home and hearth. Moon void-of-course can be a good time to take on mindless chores like cleaning house and decluttering, when we can let go of items with an almost Zen-like detachment.

Don't forget the things that you would prefer to avoid. When the Moon is void-of-course is an ideal time to do the things you really don't want to happen. Has someone has been pestering you to move a couch? Chances are if you phone during the void-of-course period you won't connect, and won't actually have to go and do it. VOC is a good time to return the multiple phone calls from that person at work. You don't want to totally blow them off because you still see them every day at the office, but chances are good during the moon void-of-course period that either you won't reach them or nothing will come of the interaction.

Consult the VOC table in the back of this book and note the dates and times on in the weekly spreads. Designate void-of-course as downtime, then remember to relax, sit back, and conserve your time, energy, money, and worry.

Now you have permission to do nothing.

December/January

31 Monday
3rd ♌
☿ enters ♑ 9:03 am
☽ v/c 4:52 pm
Color: Ivory

New Year's Eve

1 Tuesday
3rd ♌
☽ enters ♍ 12:35 pm
Color: Red

New Year's Day
Kwanzaa ends

2 Wednesday
3rd ♍
Color: Brown

Copal incense, sacred in Aztec tradition,
helps in connecting with the Divine

3 Thursday
3rd ♍
☽ v/c 7:15 am
☽ enters ♎ 8:11 pm
Color: Purple

◑ Friday
3rd ♎
4th quarter 10:58 pm
Color: White

Atho is the Finnish god of the sea,
also in charge of other waters

5 Saturday

4th ♎︎
☽ v/c 6:13 pm
Color: Gray

Oak wood traditionally fuels
Midsummer bonfires and need fires

6 Sunday

4th ♎︎
☽ enters ♏︎ 1:09 am
Color: Gold

January

7 Monday
4th ♏
☽ v/c 6:31 am
Color: Gray

8 Tuesday
4th ♏
☽ enters ♐ 3:28 am
☽ v/c 9:28 pm
♀ enters ♑ 11:11 pm
Color: Black

The angelfish represents spirit guides and the higher self

9 Wednesday
4th ♐
Color: White

Off-white represents peace of mind, calm, and receptivity

10 Thursday
4th ♐
☽ enters ♑ 3:54 am
☿ enters ♈ 12:08 pm
Color: Purple

Friday
4th ♑
☽ v/c 2:44 pm
New Moon 2:44 pm
Color: Rose

A smudging shell has air holes in the bottom,
so that a sage wand may smolder in it

Garnet

Garnet is an isometric crystal with variable mineral content. This stone comes in multiple colors, including the common almandine (reddish-purple) and the rare tsavorite (vivid green).

Magically, this stone can handle both projective and receptive energies. Its element is fire; it relates to the root and heart chakras. Mystical properties include purification, healing, and protection. Garnet enhances love, strength, and imagination. It also vitalizes and energizes the body, especially the bloodstream. On the social side, this stone supports long-term relationships and helps ensure that your path will cross with those of your friends.

In terms of protection, garnet is an ideal stone for traveling. It bolsters health on the road and defends against theft. For discreet protection, get a plain tumbled garnet bead. Fasten it to your purse, suitcase, or other traveling gear (as it protects as long as it stays in place). Then say:

Garnet wink / And garnet blink / Make the thief's ambition shrink.
Garnet glow / And garnet show / How my health will overflow.

—Elizabeth Barrette

12 Saturday

1st ♑
☽ enters ♒ 4:01 am
Color: Black

Bunbulama is an Australian goddess
who creates rain by wringing out a sponge

13 Sunday

1st ♒
☽ v/c 3:37 am
Color: Yellow

January

14 Monday

1st ≈
☽ enters ♓ 5:49 am
Color: Lavender

15 Tuesday

1st ♓
Color: Gray

Polar Bear teaches how to walk lightly over thin ice to find what you seek

16 Wednesday

1st ♓
☽ v/c 4:32 am
☽ enters ♈ 11:07 am
Color: Brown

*Brass holds defensive energy,
making it good for protective talismans*

17 Thursday

1st ♈
Color: Turquoise

○ Friday

1st ♈
2nd quarter 6:45 pm
☽ v/c 7:40 pm
☽ enters ♉ 8:36 pm
Color: Purple

For spells to increase strength, use thistle

Set in Eastern Standard Time (EST)

Imbolc: Candlelight Lemon Dessert

1 cup flour
½ cup butter
½ cup finely chopped walnuts or
  hazelnuts
2 cups frozen non-dairy whipped
  cream topping, divided
1 cup powdered sugar
8 oz. cream cheese, softened
6 oz. instant lemon pudding mix
3 cups whole milk

Imbolc is all about the soft light of spring encroaching on winter's darkness. With this soft, lemony dessert, you'll feel the glow while the lemon taste awakens your spring senses.

Several hours before serving: Combine flour, butter, and chopped nuts. Press into a 9 × 13 glass pan. Bake for 15 minutes at 350 degrees F; cool.

Combine 1 cup of the whipped topping, powdered sugar, cream cheese, and a dash of salt. Spread over the cooled crust. Chill for 15 minutes.

Combine the pudding mixes and milk; beat for about 2 minutes. Pour over the chilled mixture in the pan. Chill for 30 minutes. Top with the extra 1 cup of whipped topping. Garnish with nuts or thin lemon slices as desired. Cover tightly and chill several hours before serving. Garnish (optional).

—Susan Pesznecker

---

19 Saturday

2nd ♉
☿ enters ♒ 2:25 am
☉ enters ♒ 4:52 pm
Color: Brown

Sun enters Aquarius

---

20 Sunday

2nd ♉
☽ v/c 1:16 pm
Color: Orange

Inauguration Day

January

21 Monday
2nd ♉
☽ enters ♊ 9:04 am
Color: White

Celtic Tree Month of Rowan begins
Birthday of Martin Luther King, Jr. (observed)

22 Tuesday
2nd ♊
Color: Red

23 Wednesday
2nd ♊
☽ v/c 6:42 am
☽ enters ♋ 10:00 pm
Color: Topaz

Moth stands for keen physical and metaphysical senses

24 Thursday
2nd ♋
Color: Crimson

25 Friday
2nd ♋
☽ v/c 3:35 pm
Color: Pink

*Giving an empty purse or wallet
gives poverty, so put a coin inside*

Set in Eastern Standard Time (EST)

Cold Moon

At this time of the New Year, explore new traditions of honoring the Full Moon. Imagine the moon as your guide on a life-journey. After all, we measure our time by the Sun and Moon. Honor the Cold Moon of January by approaching the moon as though you're meeting her for the first time. Visualize a Moon goddess if you'd like. Talk to her—she's your sister, mother, grandmother, or aunt. See her as a wise witness to the ages. Let her be your mentor. No matter where you are on Earth, you can see her. Imagine a conversation you could have with her. What does she say to you? Make an offering to her on this night—light a white candle and burn sandalwood incense. Ask her to be your guiding light:

> Cold as stone, night you own
> Light for me, as I roam.
> Guiding light, in my sight
> Light for me, lead me home.
>
> —Ember Grant

☺ Saturday

2nd ♋
☽ enters ♌ 9:20 am
⚘ D 11:50 am
Full Moon 11:38 pm
Color: Indigo

Cold Moon

---

27 Sunday

3rd ♌
Color: Amber

January/February

28 Monday

3rd ♌
☽ v/c 11:59 am
☽ enters ♍ 6:27 pm
Color: Silver

Burning frankincense invokes the energy of the Sun

29 Tuesday
3rd ♍
Color: White

*Culsu is an Etruscan god who guards
the entrance to the Underworld*

30 Wednesday
3rd ♍
♃ D 6:37 am
☽ v/c 8:59 pm
Color: Yellow

31 Thursday
3rd ♍
☽ enters ♎ 1:36 am
Color: Green

1 Friday
3rd ♎
☽ v/c 8:03 pm
♂ enters ♓ 8:54 pm
♀ enters ♒ 9:47 pm
Color: White

*The yew tree is associated with death;
its wood is often used in pyres or memorial rituals*

Set in Eastern Standard Time (EST)

Imbolc

Imbolc is a time of year when spring feels far away, and we tend to focus on the coziness of hearth and home. With that in mind, work with the ancient Greek hearth goddess Hestia—the first of the gods to be invoked and the last of the gods staying in Olympus. Tonight, light a fire in the fireplace (or group several candles) and contemplate the mysteries of keeping a magickal home. In ancient times, raising a family and keeping of the home were of paramount importance. The hearth fire was all important, as it provided light and warmth. Today that hearth-fire energy may be found in the kitchen where we prepare our meals, or by the fireplace where we gather on cold winter nights. By working sabbat magic with Hestia, you honor the tradition of the sacred home and the hearth flame.

Hestia, veiled goddess of the hearth flame,
Hear me this Imbolc as I call your name.
Enchant my magickal home with warmth and light,
I await your blessings on this sabbat night.

—Ellen Dugan

---

2 Saturday

3rd ♎
☽ enters ♏ 7:02 am
Color: Gray

Imbolc
Groundhog Day

☽ Sunday

3rd ♏
4th quarter 8:56 am
Color: Orange

February

4 Monday

4th ♏
♃ D 3:48 am
☽ v/c 7:31 am
☽ enters ♐ 10:45 am
Color: Gray

Imbolc crossquarter day
(Sun reaches 15° Aquarius)

5 Tuesday

4th ♐
☿ enters ♓ 9:55 am
☽ v/c 3:42 pm
Color: White

6 Wednesday

4th ♐
☽ enters ♑ 12:55 pm
Color: Brown

The Barracuda symbolizes finding
your own way with strength and courage

7 Thursday

4th ♑
☽ v/c 7:44 am
Color: Purple

Kapo is a Hawaiian goddess in charge
of the South Pacific; she is Pele's sister

8 Friday

4th ♑
☽ enters ♒ 2:16 pm
Color: Rose

Set in Eastern Standard Time (EST)

Amethyst

Amethyst is a hexagonal crystal forming pyramids. The color is any purple, often banded with clear or white.

Historically, many folks believed amethyst protected against intoxication or poisoning. Mystical qualities include spirituality, courage, and sovereignty. Violet stones honor the Crone Goddess. Lilac ones contact higher planes. Amethyst may protect warriors, aid hunts, and improve business decisions. It can control evil thoughts.

Amethyst relaxes body and mind, granting restful sleep. It also protects against nightmares. For this, put an amethyst on your headboard. (Rinse in water each morning to remove negativity.) Charge with this incantation:

Purple crystal overhead, / Sentry set above my bed,
Let your soothing peace be spread / Where I lay my weary head.

Guide and guard me in my sleep; / Let no bad dreams make a peep.
Make all my dreams sweet and deep / As your nightly watch you keep.
—Elizabeth Barrette

---

9 Saturday

4th ≈
Color: Black

A broom made from birch twigs can sweep away evil spirits

Sunday

4th ≈
☽ v/c 2:20 am
New Moon 2:20 am
☽ enters ♓ 4:20 pm
Color: Amber

Chinese New Year (snake)

February

11 Monday

1st ♓
☽ v/c 12:03 pm
Color: White

12 Tuesday

1st ♓
☽ enters ♈ 8:51 pm
Color: Red

Mardi Gras (Fat Tuesday)

13 Wednesday
1st ♈
Color: Yellow

Ash Wednesday

14 Thursday
1st ♈
☽ v/c 10:35 pm
Color: Green

Valentine's Day

15 Friday

1st ♈
☽ enters ♉ 5:08 am
Color: Pink

Set in Eastern Standard Time (EST)

16 Saturday

1st ♉
Color: Indigo

*Cherry red is the color of intimacy
on a physical and emotional level*

☾ Sunday

1st ♉
☽ v/c 3:31 pm
2nd quarter 3:31 pm
☽ enters ♊ 4:50 pm
Color: Yellow

*The animal power of Mole
concerns introspection and grounding*

February

18 Monday

2nd ♊
☉ enters ♓ 7:02 am
♄ ℞ 12:02 pm
Color: Silver

Presidents' Day (observed)
Sun enters Pisces
Celtic Tree Month of Ash begins

19 Tuesday

2nd ♊
☽ v/c 1:48 pm
Color: Maroon

20 Wednesday

2nd ♊
☽ enters ♋ 5:45 am
Color: Topaz

*Copper transmits energy for love and luck;
wands are sometimes made of this metal*

21 Thursday

2nd ♋
☽ v/c 9:08 pm
Color: Crimson

Use mugwort when seeking prophecy

22 Friday

2nd ♋
☽ enters ♌ 5:12 pm
Color: Coral

Set in Eastern Standard Time (EST)

Jade

Jade has a monoclinic crystalline structure; it rarely forms visible crystals, often forming large masses of solid stone instead. This makes it excellent for carving into statues, talismans, jewelry, and altar tools. Precious jade is rich green, but the stone also comes in white, yellow, pink, and other colors.

This stone symbolizes love, compassion, generosity, and virtue. Its magical influences include justice, friendship, and good fortune. A strong healing stone, jade strengthens the body and protects the heart, kidneys, liver, and spleen. For personal growth, it instills resourcefulness, helping see past limitations and realize dreams. Jade aligns the physical and nonphysical planes, making it easier to travel between them and to attain desired goals.

According to Chinese tradition, jade focuses the powers of heaven. Wear a jade talisman—carved into such shapes as a dragon, goldfish, or coin—for health, wealth, and long life. Empower it with this incantation:

Jade, smooth and green, / Your force is keen.
Jade, bring me health, / Long life, and wealth.

—Elizabeth Barrette

---

23 Saturday
2nd ♌
☿ ℞ 4:41 am
Color: Brown

Praying mantis symbolizes timing, the
knowledge of exactly when and where to strike

---

24 Sunday
2nd ♌
☽ v/c 11:50 pm
Color: Gold

Purim

February/March

☺ Monday
2nd ♌
☽ enters ♍ 1:52 am
Full Moon 3:26 pm
♀ enters ♓ 9:03 pm
Color: Ivory

Quickening Moon

26 Tuesday
3rd ♍
☽ v/c 1:13 pm
Color: Black

27 Wednesday
3rd ♍
☽ enters ♎ 8:02 am
Color: White

*Sleeping in a bed that faces east makes
it easier to wake up in the morning*

28 Thursday
3rd ♎
☽ v/c 3:37 am
Color: Purple

1 Friday
3rd ♎
☽ enters ♏ 12:33 pm
Color: Purple

Musk incense boosts passion and sensuality

Set in Eastern Standard Time (EST)

Quickening Moon

The Quickening Moon is a time of subtle awakening. There is a stirring in the land, barely recognizable. Honor this month's Full Moon by making time to clear the way for a new season—make plans for the future. Write a goal or project you hope to complete on a piece of paper and burn a white candle on top of it (in a safe container, or on a plate). Make a promise to yourself or pledge your effort to a project, life-

style change, or other goal. The Moon is your witness. In August, revisit this goal and check your progress. If you'd like, dedicate a piece of jewelry during this ritual; something you can wear as a reminder of your goal. Burn incense of myrrh, sage, spikenard, or a combination of these and chant as you visualize your goal:

> *Constant Moon*
> *Quicken my heart,*
> *Quicken my blood,*
> *This is the start.*
> —Ember Grant

---

2 Saturday

3rd ♏
Color: Gray

Janus is the Roman god of doors
and also presides over the turning year

---

3 Sunday

3rd ♏
☽ v/c 4:19 am
☽ enters ♐ 4:11 pm
Color: Yellow

March

◑ Monday
3rd ♐
4th quarter 4:53 pm
Color: Lavender

5 Tuesday
4th ♐
☽ v/c 10:28 am
☽ enters ♑ 7:14 pm
Color: Gray

The Rowan tree has healing and protective powers

6 Wednesday
4th ♑
Color: Topaz

Coral represents a solid foundation to build upon

7 Thursday
4th ♑
☽ v/c 4:14 pm
☽ enters ♒ 10:01 pm
Color: Turquoise

Gauari is the Hindu goddess of purity and austerity

8 Friday
4th ♒
☽ v/c 5:08 pm
Color: Rose

9 Saturday

4th ≈
Color: Brown

10 Sunday

4th ≈
☽ enters ♓ 1:19 am
Color: Orange

Daylight Saving Time begins at 2 am

March

☽ Monday
4th ♓
☽ v/c 3:51 pm
New Moon 3:51 pm
Color: White

A scrying mirror is a special tool made from dark glass,
obsidian, or onyx that may reveal mystical visions

12 Tuesday
1st ♓
♂ enters ♈ 2:26 am
☽ enters ♈ 7:17 am
Color: Black

13 Wednesday
1st ♈
⚸ enters ♒ 3:12 am
☽ v/c 4:02 am
Color: Brown

Rose-pink is a healing color,
especially for emotional injuries

14 Thursday
1st ♈
☽ enters ♉ 3:08 pm
Color: Green

15 Friday
1st ♉
Color: Pink

A Lynx totem deals in the unseen, the secret, and the mysterious

Set in Eastern Daylight Time (EDT)

Creamed Peas and New Potatoes

2 lbs. scrubbed new potatoes (or
  fingerling potatoes from the store)
2 T. butter
2 T. flour
1½ cup whole milk, room temp.
⅛ tsp. nutmeg (preferably
  fresh-grated)
1 cup shelled peas, fresh

Cook the potatoes (peeled if you prefer) in boiling salted water for about 10
minutes or until just tender. Add the
peas during the last minute of cooking.
Drain, immerse in cold water to chill and stop the cooking. Set aside.

In a three-quart saucepan, melt the butter over medium heat until bub-
bly. Stir in the flour and cook for 3 to 4 minutes, stirring frequently—don't
allow the mixture to brown.

Remove the pan from the heat and whisk in the milk, blending well.

Return the pan to the burner and heat, stirring very frequently, until
the mixture boils and thickens. Then stir in the nutmeg. Taste the white
sauce; add salt and pepper to taste. If the sauce seems thick, stir in a bit more
milk. Add the potatoes and peas and heat gently until warmed through.

—Susan Pesznecker

16 Saturday

1st ♉
☽ v/c 7:11 pm
Color: Black

17 Sunday

1st ♉
☽ enters ♊ 2:09 am
☿ D 4:03 pm
Color: Gold

St. Patrick's Day

March

18 Monday
1st ♊
Color: Gray

Celtic Tree Month of Alder begins

◗ Tuesday
1st ♊
☽ v/c 1:27 pm
2nd quarter 1:27 pm
☽ enters ♋ 2:55 pm
Color: Red

---

20 Wednesday
2nd ♋
☉ enters ♈ 7:02 am
☽ v/c 2:02 pm
Color: White

Ostara/Spring Equinox
Sun enters Aries
International Astrology Day

---

21 Thursday
2nd ♋
♀ enters ♈ 11:15 pm
Color: Purple

---

22 Friday
2nd ♋
☽ enters ♌ 2:50 am
☽ v/c 11:28 pm
Color: Coral

*Electrum is a blend of metals,
representing the balance between
masculine and feminine energies*

Set in Eastern Daylight Time (EDT)

Ostara

Finally, winter is losing its grip on the land and life is starting to emerge. But this season is wild and untamed. One day may be warm and springlike, but the next could dump one last shot of snow. Nature keeps us guessing, and we will never tame her energy. With that in mind, the Greek Goddess of the Hunt, Artemis, is a perfect deity to work with on this sabbat. The eternal Virgin, the untamed, wild, and free huntress of the forests

and of the night. Associated with the Moon, fertility, and childbirth, Artemis protects the wild, unspoiled places in nature and is naturally connected with the growing season. Her symbol, the waxing crescent Moon, is visible in the night sky right now. So call upon Artemis and allow her to bring her movement, courage, and a sense of freedom into your celebration of the spring.

Artemis, the brave and wild huntress, hear my cry,
Your symbol, the waxing Moon shines down from the sky
Eternal Maiden, you represent fertility,
At the Vernal Equinox, send your blessings to me.

—Ellen Dugan

23 Saturday
2nd ♌
Color: Blue

For prosperity, use sunflower seeds

24 Sunday
2nd ♌
☽ enters ♍ 11:49 am
Color: Amber

Palm Sunday

March

25 Monday
2nd ♍
☽ v/c 8:46 am
Color: Silver

Spider represents patience and craftsmanship

26 Tuesday
2nd ♍
☽ enters ♎ 5:32 pm
Color: Maroon

Passover begins

☺ Wednesday
2nd ♎
Full Moon 5:27 am
☽ v/c 2:14 pm
Color: Yellow

Storm Moon

28 Thursday
3rd ♎
☽ enters ♏ 8:53 pm
Color: Green

29 Friday
3rd ♏
☽ v/c 4:25 pm
Color: White

Good Friday

Set in Eastern Daylight Time (EDT)

Storm Moon

This month can bring turbulent times as the land begins to awaken with the coming spring. Embrace a sense of calm as you welcome the Storm Moon by performing a bath ritual. First, prepare an infusion of apple by steeping slices of apple in hot water until the water is cool; then remove the pieces. Add a few drops of honeysuckle essential oil to the infusion and allow it to sit in the moonlight for as long as you like. If possible, add a bit of fresh rainwater (or melted snow) as well. Visualize the moonlight charging the infusion with energy. This energy is soft, but powerful; gentle, yet persistent. When you're ready, add this infusion to your bath. Alternatively, you can use the infusion in the shower, if you don't have a tub. As you wash, cleanse yourself with moonlight.

> *Full Moon wrapped in sky's embrace*
> *Full Moon, wash me in your grace*
> *Light cascading from your face*
> *Set me free from time and place.*
> —Ember Grant

---

30 Saturday

3rd ♏︎
♀ enters ♉︎ 7:40 am
☽ enters ♐︎ 11:13 pm
Color: Indigo

Henna designs on hands and feet convey protection

---

31 Sunday

3rd ♐︎
Color: Yellow

Easter

April

1 Monday

3rd ♐
☽ v/c 1:00 am
Color: White

April Fools' Day (All Fools' Day—Pagan)

2 Tuesday

3rd ♐
☽ enters ♑ 1:35 am
Color: Black

Passover ends

◑ Wednesday

3rd ♑
4th quarter 12:37 am
☽ v/c 6:35 am
Color: Yellow

4 Thursday

4th ♑
☽ enters ♒ 4:41 am
♀ enters ♋ 6:17 pm
Color: Crimson

Burn myrrh for protection and purification

5 Friday

4th ♒
☽ v/c 1:22 pm
Color: Rose

6 Saturday

4th ♒
☽ enters ♓ 9:00 am
Color: Blue

Latis is the Celtic goddess who oversees water and beer

7 Sunday

4th ♓
Color: Orange

*The ash tree is associated
with the sea holding power over water*

April

8 Monday

4th ♓

☽ v/c 12:10 am

☽ enters ♈ 3:02 pm

Color: Silver

Dolphin symbolizes creativity, play, and curiosity

9 Tuesday

4th ♈

Color: Maroon

☽ Wednesday

4th ♈

New Moon 5:35 am

☽ v/c 12:25 pm

☽ enters ♉ 11:22 pm

Color: White

*Raluvhimba is an
African creator god,
lord of the heavens*

11 Thursday

1st ♉

Color: Purple

*A pendulum is a pointed stone or other
weight on a chain used for divination*

12 Friday

1st ♉

♇ ℞ 3:34 pm

Color: Pink

Set in Eastern Daylight Time (EDT)

Moonstone

Moonstone is a monoclinic crystal. This stone has various colors including white, silvery gray, yellow, orange, brown, bluish, and pink. Tumbled chunks or polished cabochons show off its iridescence.

Ancient Romans believed moonlight formed moonstone, using it in sacred jewelry. It's sacred in India too. For healing, moonstone reminds vertebrae to stay aligned and aids digestion. It buffers emotions, balancing yin/yang energies. For lovers, moonstone (13th anniversary stone) evokes romantic tenderness rather than intense passion. This stone symbolizes Moon, sea, and planting cycles. However, moonstone's greatest power is protecting mothers and babies. Pregnant women may wear a moonstone amulet on a silver chain—try to find a goddess pendant with a moonstone belly. Begin with this charm (and recharge the amulet under the light of a Full Moon):

Stone of the Moon / Grant me a boon,
And so vouchsafe / To keep us safe,
My babe and me / By Moon and Sea.

—Elizabeth Barrette

---

13 Saturday

1st ♉
☽ v/c 8:30 am
☽ enters ♊ 10:13 am
☿ enters ♈ 10:37 pm
Color: Brown

---

14 Sunday

1st ♊
Color: Gold

Deep pink invites harmony and friendship into the home

April

15 Monday
1st ♊
♀ enters ♉ 3:25 am
☽ v/c 3:41 pm
☽ enters ♋ 10:49 pm
Color: Lavender

Celtic Tree Month of Willow begins

16 Tuesday
1st ♋
Color: White

17 Wednesday
1st ♋
Color: Topaz

Working with Jaguar enhances spiritual and psychic awareness

◐ Thursday
1st ♋
☽ v/c 8:31 am
2nd quarter 8:31 am
☽ enters ♌ 11:13 am
Color: Turquoise

19 Friday
2nd ♌
☽ v/c 5:06 pm
☉ enters ♉ 6:03 pm
Color: Purple

Sun enters Taurus

Set in Eastern Daylight Time (EDT)

Sexy Spicy Chicken Wings

3–4 lbs chicken wings
⅓ cup molasses
⅓ cup soy sauce or tamari
2 T. fresh lemon juice
¾ tsp. dried ginger
1 inch fresh ginger root, peeled
   and grated
½ tsp. dry mustard
2 T. chopped onion
¼ tsp. red pepper flakes
½ to 1 tsp. Sriracha sauce (a Thai
   chili pepper–based condiment)

Chicken wings have three sections: Snip off the tough little end section and freeze to use later when making chicken stock. Cut each remaining wing into two pieces at the joint. Then combine all of the ingredients—including the wings—in a heavy zippered plastic freezer bag. Allow to marinate 4 to 5 hours or overnight, turning occasionally.

When ready to cook, drain completely. Bake, skin-side up, at 400 degrees F on a foil-covered baking sheet for 30 to 35 minutes. These savory and juicy wings have a combination of "sweet and heat" that makes them a perfect Beltaine snack. They'll disappear before you can say "maypole!"

—Susan Pesznecker

20 Saturday

2nd ♌
♂ enters ♉ 7:48 am
☽ enters ♍ 9:08 pm
Color: Black

Wear gold jewelry to attract success and wealth

21 Sunday

2nd ♍
Color: Amber

Sweet marjoram aids in love spells

April

22 Monday
2nd ♍
☽ v/c 2:02 am
Color: Gray

Earth Day; the first Earth Day was in 1970

23 Tuesday
2nd ♍
☽ enters ♎ 3:25 am
Color: Red

Paper wasp signifies productivity and construction

24 Wednesday
2nd ♎
☽ v/c 8:12 am
♀ enters ♋ 8:48 pm
Color: White

☺ Thursday

2nd ♎
☽ enters ♏ 6:25 am
Full Moon 3:57 pm
Color: Green

Wind Moon
Lunar eclipse 4:07 pm, 5° ♏ 51'

26 Friday

3rd ♏
☽ v/c 4:56 am
Color: Coral

Set in Eastern Daylight Time (EDT)

Wind Moon

Look at the Moon tonight; hopefully, you can see it. If there are clouds, watch the way they move across the Moon's face. Lose yourself in this for a moment. The Moon is far removed from our atmosphere, but sometimes we forget because the wind seems to sweep across its surface. But all is still and calm on the Moon. This is a centering ritual for times when things are unsettled—picture yourself like the Moon, distant from our atmosphere, the wind is far away; you remain untouched.

Winds that blow, far below
Cannot touch, never know
I am safe beyond the reach
Of any harm or any breach.
I am calm and I am still
In any wind, come what will.
                                    —Ember Grant

---

27 Saturday
3rd ♏
☽ enters ♐ 7:32 am
Color: Indigo

---

28 Sunday
3rd ♐
Color: Yellow

Adding milk to a bath purifies and nourishes

April/May

29 Monday

3rd ♐
☽ v/c 12:37 am
☽ enters ♑ 8:21 am
Color: Ivory

*Patchouli incense has an earthy
scent, good for physical attraction*

30 Tuesday

3rd ♑
Color: Gray

Utu is the Sumerian sun god, also in charge of justice

1 Wednesday

3rd ♑
☽ v/c 10:07 am
☽ enters ♒ 10:20 am
☿ enters ♉ 11:37 am
Color: Brown

Beltane/May Day

○ Thursday

3rd ♒
4th quarter 7:14 am
Color: Turquoise

3 Friday

3rd ♒
☽ v/c 12:24 am
☽ enters ♓ 2:25 pm
Color: White

Orthodox Good Friday

Set in Eastern Daylight Time (EDT)

Beltane

The lusty celebration of Beltane is upon us! Gardens bloom and wild places are leafy and green. Weather is mild and thoughts turn to passion. In garden folklore, any blue flower—violets, periwinkles, soft bluish-purple tulips, and early hydrangeas—is sacred to the Greek goddess Aphrodite. This Beltane, work with her to send a little passion and romance your way. Remember, Aphrodite does not bring lasting love into your life…she brings attraction, romance, passion, and physical love. This is great for established partners to spice things up or singles looking for a new someone for romance. To work with Aphrodite's energy, gather a few blue flowers from the garden and tie them with a satin ribbon. Slip the flowers in a water-filled vessel and offer them to Aphrodite along with this spell verse for Beltane.

On the feast of Beltane, I'll try a little something new,
I request Aphrodite's blessings with flowers of blue.
Passion and fun, you will surely bring to my life,
May I be blessed with magick and romance on this night.

—Ellen Dugan

---

4 Saturday

4th ♓
Color: Gray

---

5 Sunday

4th ♓
☽ v/c 12:00 pm
☽ enters ♈ 9:03 pm
Color: Gold

Cinco de Mayo
Orthodox Easter
Beltane crossquarter day
(Sun reaches 15° Taurus)

May

6 Monday
4th ♈
Color: Gray

7 Tuesday
4th ♈
☽ v/c 8:40 am
Color: White

The pine tree is androgynous,
a good choice for two-spirited practitioners

8 Wednesday
4th ♈
☽ enters ♉ 6:09 am
Color: Topaz

☽ Thursday
4th ♉
♀ enters ♊ 11:03 am
☽ v/c 8:28 pm
New Moon 8:28 pm
Color: Purple

Solar eclipse 10:55 pm, 19° ♉ 33'

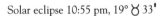

10 Friday
1st ♉
☽ enters ♊ 5:21 pm
Color: Coral

Census Day (Canada)

Set in Eastern Daylight Time (EDT)

11 Saturday

1st ♊
Color: Indigo

The frog stands for transformation and duality

12 Sunday

1st ♊
☽ v/c 9:32 am
Color: Orange

Mother's Day

May

13 Monday

1st ♊
☽ enters ♋ 5:57 am
Color: White

Celtic Tree Month of Hawthorn begins

14 Tuesday

1st ♋
Color: Gray

Use a marble mortar and pestle for grinding
magical herbs to add extra power for spellcraft

15 Wednesday

1st ♋
☽ v/c 8:14 am
☿ enters ♊ 4:41 pm
☽ enters ♌ 6:38 pm
Color: Brown

Shavuot

16 Thursday

1st ♌
Color: Crimson

Sengen-Sama is a Japanese goddess,
dwelling in the sacred mountain Fujiyama

17 Friday

1st ♌
Color: Rose

Set in Eastern Daylight Time (EDT)

Agate

Agate crystals typically form in banded or layered masses with microfibrous structure. Colors include white, brown, red, yellow, and green; a single stone often bears multiple colors in stripes or spots. Soft and good for carving, agates can be made into amulets, seals, jewelry, and containers. Magically, agate improves memory, vitality, and hearing. It grants courage and self-confidence, helping to overcome addictive behaviors. Various

agates have their own qualities. Banded agate balances bodily energies and relieves stress. Moss agate is a gardeners talisman. Red agate guards against spider and insect bites. Yellow agate activates creativity and inspiration.

Ancient people believed that eye beads would ward against evil and attract good fortune. Even today, it is possible to find eye beads carved from agate. These protective talismans make the wearer "invisible" to danger or malicious energy, especially the "evil eye." Empower one with this chant:

Eye blink / And eye stare: / To danger, nothing's there.
Eye wink / And eye glare: / So leave me free of care.

—Elizabeth Barrette

○ Saturday

1st ♌
☽ v/c 12:35 am
2nd quarter 12:35 am
☽ enters ♍ 5:33 am
Color: Black

---

19 Sunday

2nd ♍
Color: Amber

Peach is the color of trust, useful in spells
for establishing or restoring connections

May

20 Monday
2nd ♍
☽ v/c 12:48 pm
☽ enters ♎ 1:07 pm
☉ enters ♊ 5:09 pm
Color: Silver

Sun enters Gemini

21 Tuesday
2nd ♎
Color: Black

Connect with Hedgehog to learn about tenacity and defense

22 Wednesday
2nd ♎
☽ v/c 3:35 am
☽ enters ♏ 4:55 pm
Color: White

*Iron manifests protection through
strength, especially in emblems of weaponry*

23 Thursday
2nd ♏
Color: Green

24 Friday
2nd ♏
☽ v/c 9:55 am
☽ enters ♐ 5:49 pm
Color: Pink

High John the Conqueror root is helpful with legal issues

Set in Eastern Daylight Time (EDT)

Flower Moon

What is blooming around you? Gather a bundle of herbs, flowers, and leaves, and tie them with several ribbons in various colors—be sure to include red and white. Put the bouquet in a vase of water. This is a fertile season—celebrate by decorating your altar or other special place with this bundle and candles to represent the fire of passion. Focus on stirring or rekindling a relationship, if you wish. To do this, add a symbol of the relationship to your altar and surround it with the bouquet and candles. Visualize the fire and flowers infusing your relationship with a spark.

Loving light, fragrant blooms,
Celebrate the Flower Moon.
Dance around, stir the fire—
Fan the flames of desire.

—Ember Grant

Saturday

2nd ♐
Full Moon 12:25 am
Color: Brown

Flower Moon
Lunar eclipse 12:10 am, 3° ♐ 58'

26 Sunday

3rd ♐
☽ v/c 6:22 am
☽ enters ♑ 5:28 pm
Color: Yellow

May

27 Monday
3rd ♑
Color: Ivory

Memorial Day (observed)

28 Tuesday
3rd ♑
☽ v/c 2:40 pm
☽ enters ♒ 5:48 pm
♀ enters ♊ 11:09 pm
Color: Maroon

Ant symbolizes social structure and industriousness

29 Wednesday
3rd ♒
Color: Topaz

30 Thursday
3rd ♒
☽ v/c 7:57 pm
☽ enters ♓ 8:30 pm
Color: Turquoise

Dropping silverware predicts a guest:
fork for a man, spoon for a woman

○ Friday
3rd ♓
☿ enters ♋ 3:07 am
♂ enters ♊ 6:39 am
4th quarter 2:58 pm
Color: Purple

Set in Eastern Daylight Time (EDT)

1 Saturday

4th ♓

Color: Brown

2 Sunday

4th ♓

☽ v/c 12:30 am
☽ enters ♈ 2:33 am
♀ enters ♋ 10:13 pm

Color: Amber

Burn sandalwood for healing and regeneration

June

3 Monday

4th ♈
Color: Lavender

4 Tuesday

4th ♈
☽ v/c 2:09 am
☽ enters ♉ 11:53 am
Color: Scarlet

Frey is the Norse god of fertility and abundance

5 Wednesday

4th ♉
☽ v/c 9:25 am
Color: Yellow

6 Thursday

4th ♉
☽ enters ♊ 11:32 pm
Color: Green

The willow tree has strong female energy associated with the Moon

7 Friday

4th ♊
♆ ℞ 4:24 am
Color: Pink

Set in Eastern Daylight Time (EDT)

Stuffed Zucchini

6 medium zucchini (or 1–2 giants)
½ cup butter
2 T. chopped onion
4 oz. canned mushrooms, drained
2 T. ketchup
½ tsp. salt
Dash of nutmeg and black pepper
Dash of Worcestershire sauce
¾ cup cracker crumbs
¼ cup grated Parmesan cheese
1 T. butter, melted

Slice zucchini in half, lengthwise, i.e., making "zucchini boats." Scoop out the center of each, finely chop the removed material, and set aside.

Sauté onion in ½ cup butter until softened. Slice then add mushrooms and cook another 3 to 4 minutes. Stir in chopped squash mixture, ketchup, salt, nutmeg, pepper, Worcestershire sauce, and cracker crumbs.

Use this mixture to stuff the squash boats. Sprinkle with Parmesan, and drizzle with melted butter. Put the squashes into a large baking dish. Pour ½ cup water into the pan around them. Cover with foil and bake at 350 degrees F for 20 minutes. Remove foil and bake for 25 to 30 more minutes, until done.

—Susan Pesznecker

☽ Saturday
4th ♊
New Moon 11:56 am
Color: Gray

9 Sunday
1st ♊
☽ v/c 4:29 am
☽ enters ♋ 12:16 pm
Color: Yellow

Eos is the Greek goddess of dawn,
in charge of light and beginnings

June

10 Monday

1st ♋
☽ v/c 5:15 pm
Color: Ivory

Celtic Tree Month of Oak begins

11 Tuesday

1st ♋
Color: Black

Goldfish represents prosperity and peace

12 Wednesday

1st ♋
☽ enters ♌ 12:58 am
Color: White

13 Thursday

1st ♌
Color: Purple

The asperger, or aspergillium,
is a device for sprinkling blessed water

14 Friday

1st ♌
☽ v/c 7:14 am
☽ enters ♍ 12:26 pm
Color: Rose

Flag Day

Set in Eastern Daylight Time (EDT)

Midsummer

The Summer Solstice has arrived. All of nature is busy growing and blooming, but in the summer months thunderstorms also rip across the land. Working with Zeus, Greek king of the gods, is a great way to bring wisdom, power, and success to your magick. The oak tree, the eagle, and the metal gold are all associated with Zeus, and so is the lightning bolt. As oak trees are prominent in classic Summer Solstice rituals, take a few oak leaves and scat-

ter them across your altar. Add a yellow candle for the Sun and carve a lightning bolt for Zeus into the candle. Place the candle in the holder, light it, and work this spell to create positive change. Magick in the air tonight.

Zeus I ask for your blessing on this enchanted night,
I see your mighty power in the lightning that strikes.
These green oak leaves bring wisdom and prosperity,
May these gifts come swiftly and surely now to me.
Grant success, happiness, and knowledge to me I pray,
As I celebrate the magick of the longest day.

—Ellen Dugan

15 Saturday
1st ♍
✷ ℞ 2:42 am
Color: Indigo

☽ Sunday
1st ♍
☿ ℞ 5:17 am
2nd quarter 1:24 pm
☽ v/c 5:26 pm
☽ enters ♎ 9:19 pm
Color: Gold

Father's Day

June

17 Monday
2nd ♎︎
Color: Gray

Red-orange represents failure,
helpful in recovering from mistakes

18 Tuesday
2nd ♎︎
☽ v/c 11:55 pm
Color: Red

19 Wednesday
2nd ♎︎
☽ enters ♏︎ 2:38 am
Color: Brown

A Giraffe totem
corresponds to farsightedness
and balance between earth and sky

20 Thursday
2nd ♏︎
☽ v/c 3:16 pm
Color: Turquoise

21 Friday
2nd ♏︎
☉ enters ♋︎ 1:04 am
☽ enters ♐︎ 4:31 am
Color: White

Sun enters Cancer
Midsummer/Litha/Summer Solstice

Strong Sun Moon

The month of the Summer Solstice celebrates the Strong Sun Moon. It's easy to forget that the Moon glows by borrowed light from the Sun. To celebrate this Full Moon, rejoice in the lushness of midsummer. Make a bonfire or, if that's not possible, use a small cauldron to burn some aromatic herbs (such as lavender, yarrow, vervain) or oak leaves and branches. If you have a fire pit on your patio, you can add herbs to that fire. Honor the life-giving light that the Sun shares with us in the darkness, by way of the Moon's reflection. Use this chant as you light your fire beneath the moonlight:

Moon kissed by midsummer Sun,
Strongest light can now become
Energy for night and day—
Light of life to lead our way.
                    —Ember Grant

---

22 Saturday
2nd ♐
♃ enters ♌ 8:13 am
Color: Blue

☺ Sunday
2nd ♐
☽ v/c 3:08 am
☽ enters ♑ 4:08 am
Full Moon 7:32 am
Color: Orange

June

24 Monday

3rd ♑
☽ v/c 10:24 pm
Color: White

25 Tuesday

3rd ♑
☽ enters ♒ 3:27 am
♃ enters ♋ 9:40 pm
Color: Gray

Lodestone is a powerful attractor for any goal

26 Wednesday

3rd ♒
☿ ℞ 9:08 am
☽ v/c 9:08 am
Color: Topaz

For healing magic, use wintergreen or peppermint

27 Thursday

3rd ♒
☽ enters ♓ 4:32 am
♀ enters ♌ 1:03 pm
Color: Crimson

28 Friday

3rd ♓
☽ v/c 8:16 pm
Color: Coral

Beetles represent transformation and resurrection

Set in Eastern Daylight Time (EDT)

Chalcedony

Chalcedony is cryptocrystalline with waxy luster, semitransparent or translucent. Colors are white, gray, brown, or multicolored. Jewelers prize a moon-blue shade. Mystically, chalcedony extends vitality, physical stamina, emotional endurance. It fosters peace, encouraging honesty. This reduces negative emotions. For healing, it deals with fever, gallstones, and vision. Its gentle energy balances mind-body-spirit.

Blue chalcedony makes altar images for air/water. It can influence weather. For this, use a chalcedony cameo with a face on it or a tumbled stone in the shape of a cloud. Attune with these words:

Blue as the sky / So clear and high
Rule over air / So fine and fair
Rule water too / So deep and blue
By magic's will / No weather ill

For calm weather, charge it on a clear day. To bring rain, charge on a stormy day.

—Elizabeth Barrette

---

29 Saturday

3rd ♓
☽ enters ♈ 9:07 am
Color: Brown

Avoid sweeping dirt out the door, lest the luck of the house go with it

---

☽ Sunday

3rd ♈
4th quarter 12:54 am
Color: Yellow

July

1 Monday
4th ♈
☽ v/c 2:48 am
☽ enters ♉ 5:43 pm
Color: Silver

Amber incense brings comfort and peace

2 Tuesday
4th ♉
Color: White

The elder tree is associated with
magical power and control over mystical energies

3 Wednesday
4th ♉
☽ v/c 11:51 am
Color: Yellow

4 Thursday
4th ♉
☽ enters ♊ 5:21 am
Color: Green

Independence Day

5 Friday
4th ♊
Color: Purple

Set in Eastern Daylight Time (EDT)

6 Saturday

4th ♊

♅ enters ♌ 5:59 am

☽ v/c 8:30 am

☽ enters ♋ 6:14 pm

Color: Black

7 Sunday

4th ♋

Color: Gold

Hypnos is the Greek god of sleep,
Morpheus the god of dreams;
call on them for help with insomnia

July

☽ Monday
4th ♋
♄ D 1:12 am
New Moon 3:14 am
☽ v/c 7:44 am
Color: Gray

Celtic Tree Month of Holly begins

9 Tuesday
1st ♋
☽ enters ♌ 6:48 am
Color: Black

Ramadan begins

10 Wednesday
1st ♌
Color: White

11 Thursday
1st ♌
☽ v/c 3:54 pm
☽ enters ♍ 6:12 pm
Color: Crimson

The Jellyfish symbolizes simplicity and trust; go with the flow

12 Friday
1st ♍
Color: Rose

Set in Eastern Daylight Time (EDT)

Turquoise

Turquoise occasionally forms tri-clinic crystals, usually appearing in rounded nuggets or large smooth masses that may be carved. Small nuggets are often left whole for beads. This stone has shades of pale blue to blue-green, and rarely apple-green. Turquoise relates to Jupiter and Venus.

This stone relates to the sky and the element of air. Mystical qualities include happiness, health, and spirituality. It absorbs danger and defends from falling. As a decoration on weapons, it improves eyesight and aim. A good weather stone, it can predict storms and protect against lightning. Keep a chunk of turquoise in its native matrix in your home to stop arguments, relieve anger, and promote peace. Turquoise relates to goddesses of love across multiple cultures, such as Aphrodite (Greek), Isis (Egyptian), and Venus (Roman). This stone fosters "true blue" love based on loyalty and affection rather than lust. A good charm for couples is to wear matching pieces of turquoise jewelry. Attune them with this chant:

True and blue / Two by two / See us through / Me and you.

—Elizabeth Barrette

---

13 Saturday

1st ♍︎
♂ enters ♋ 9:22 am
☽ v/c 11:26 am
Color: Brown

Skadi is the Norse goddess of winter;
she aids hunters when snow is on the ground

---

14 Sunday

1st ♍︎
☽ enters ♎ 3:41 am
Color: Yellow

July

◑ Monday
1st ♎︎
☽ v/c 11:18 pm
2nd quarter 11:18 pm
Color: White

16 Tuesday
2nd ♎︎
☽ enters ♏︎ 10:24 am
Color: Red

*A candle snuffer is a useful altar tool, often
decorated with water imagery as the opposite of fire*

17 Wednesday
2nd ♏︎
♅ ℞ 1:20 pm
Color: Topaz

18 Thursday
2nd ♏︎
☽ v/c 7:12 am
☽ enters ♐︎ 1:54 pm
Color: Green

*Sunshine-yellow stands for a new home,
useful both in house-hunting and home blessings*

19 Friday
2nd ♐︎
Color: Coral

Peachy Libations

Peach Bellini:
½ cup sugar
½ cup water
2 large ripe peaches
1 bottle Champagne or Prosecco
Fresh mint leaves

Several hours before serving: combine sugar and water in a saucepan. Bring to a boil, stirring to dissolve sugar. Cool and chill in refrigerator. This is your simple syrup.

Before serving: peel and pit the peaches, cutting out blemishes. Puree the peaches with ¼ cup simple syrup. Taste. Add more syrup if needed.

Fill a champagne flute about a one-third full with the peach mixture. Fill the rest with Champagne, stirring gently to combine. Garnish with mint leaves.

Peach Fuzzie: Combine 2 ripe peaches (pit and cut out blemishes), 6 ounces frozen lemonade or limeade concentrate, 6 ounces gin or vodka, and 1 cup crushed ice in a blender and blend until slushy. Serve in chilled glasses; add a straw and garnish with lemon or lime wedges and mint leaves.

The perfectly ripened peach is a precious seasonal treat. Enjoy!

—Susan Pesznecker

---

20 Saturday

2nd ♐
☽ v/c 11:00 am
☿ D 2:22 pm
☽ enters ♑ 2:39 pm
Color: Gray

---

21 Sunday

2nd ♑
♀ enters ♋ 9:00 am
☽ v/c 11:53 am
Color: Amber

Fox has the animal power of walking between worlds and seeing possibilities

July

☺ Monday

2nd ♑
♀ enters ♍ 8:41 am
☉ enters ♌ 11:56 am
☽ enters ♒ 2:07 pm
Full Moon 2:16 pm
Color: Lavender

Blessing Moon
Sun enters Leo

23 Tuesday

3rd ♒
☽ v/c 10:01 am
Color: Gray

24 Wednesday

3rd ♒
☽ enters ♓ 2:22 pm
Color: Brown

*Silver connects with feminine energy and the
Goddess, particularly when charged with moonlight*

25 Thursday

3rd ♓
☽ v/c 2:43 pm
Color: Purple

26 Friday

3rd ♓
☽ enters ♈ 5:29 pm
Color: Pink

Star anise brings luck

Blessing Moon

For the July Full Moon, explore your intuitive gifts. One way to gain this insight is through your dreams. Charge a silver charm or a stone that you can tuck into your pillow or under your mattress, or make a dream pillow stuffed with lavender, jasmine, or honeysuckle. If you prefer, use aromatherapy and breathe the scent of these flowers in essential oil form. Meditate before going to sleep, and focus on receiving insight from your dreams. But remember that restful sleep is important, so focus on your dreams being peaceful and not disruptive.

By light of Moon my dreams are clear
The goddess whispers in my ear
By light of Moon my sleep is blessed
And I will wake from peaceful rest.
　　　　　　　　　—Ember Grant

---

27 Saturday
3rd ♈
☽ v/c 10:19 pm
Color: Indigo

Cicada stands for hidden knowledge and power over illusions

---

28 Sunday
3rd ♈
Color: Orange

July/August

○ Monday
3rd ♈
☽ enters ♉ 12:43 am
4th quarter 1:43 pm
Color: White

30 Tuesday
4th ♉
☽ v/c 11:58 am
Color: Black

*If you borrow salt, pay it back with
sugar to encourage a sweet relationship*

31 Wednesday
4th ♉
☽ enters ♊ 11:42 am
Color: Yellow

1 Thursday
4th ♊
☽ v/c 12:48 pm
Color: Purple

Lammas/Lughnasadh

2 Friday
4th ♊
Color: White

Lammas

Heat covers the land in shimmering waves, the days are bright and intense, and the gardens and fields are yielding their first crops and fruits. Today we celebrate the first of our three harvest festivals. Let's work with Demeter, the ancient goddess of the harvest and agriculture. Her symbols include red poppies, wheat, and grains (and garden-grown produce). If you don't have the space to grow vegetables at home, take a trip to the local farmers' market and pick up some seasonal goodies. Look for varieties of heirloom tomatoes, peaches, squash, peppers, sweet corn, and new potatoes. Take these home and conjure up something fresh and healthy to celebrate the first harvest with your loved ones, coven, and friends. Here is a spell that calls on Demeter and asks for her blessings, and for abundance.

> *At this first harvest, may all of the crops grow strong and true,*
> *Home garden or farmer's field, for your bounty, we thank you.*
> *Demeter, goddess of the harvest, protect us all we pray,*
> *May we be blessed with abundance and health for all of our days.*
>
> —Ellen Dugan

---

3 Saturday

4th ♊
☽ enters ♋ 12:29 am
Color: Black

Burn benzoin to release negative energy and harsh emotions

---

4 Sunday

4th ♋
Color: Gold

Ch'eng Huang is the Chinese god of walls and moats, overseeing all to do with barriers

---

August

5 Monday

4th ♋
☽ v/c 2:49 am
☽ enters ♌ 12:58 pm
Color: Silver

Celtic Tree Month of Hazel begins

☽ Tuesday

4th ♌
☽ v/c 5:51 pm
New Moon 5:51 pm
Color: Red

7 Wednesday

1st ♌
☽ enters ♍ 11:57 pm
Color: White

Ramadan ends
Lammas crossquarter day
(Sun reaches 15° Leo)

8 Thursday

1st ♍
☿ enters ♌ 8:13 am
Color: Turquoise

9 Friday

1st ♍
☽ v/c 6:05 pm
Color: Pink

Lobster represents camouflage and protection

Set in Eastern Daylight Time (EDT)

10 Saturday

1st ♍

☽ enters ♎ 9:08 am

Color: Indigo

The hawthorn tree, representing the White Goddess,
has thorns for powerful protection

11 Sunday

1st ♎

☽ v/c 9:29 pm

Color: Yellow

August

12 Monday

1st ♎
☽ enters ♏ 4:18 pm
Color: White

Nammu is the Sumerian goddess of the sea and all its treasures

13 Tuesday

1st ♏
Color: Gray

◐ Wednesday

1st ♏
2nd quarter 6:56 am
☽ v/c 5:30 pm
☽ enters ♐ 9:04 pm
Color: Topaz

Spring-green relates to fertility and children

15 Thursday

2nd ♐
Color: Green

*A candleholder in a symbolic shape can direct energy,
thereby reducing the need for expensive colored candles*

16 Friday

2nd ♐
♀ enters ♎ 11:37 am
☽ v/c 1:32 pm
☽ enters ♑ 11:25 pm
Color: Purple

Set in Eastern Daylight Time (EDT)

Carnelian

Carnelian has a hexagonal crystal system and often appears in solid masses rather than prisms. Popular for carving into rings or seals, it also makes fine cabochons. Colors range from yellow to brown with reddish-orange prevailing; stones may be solidly colored or streaked.

Magically, this stone calms the temper by absorbing anger and negative emotions. It strengthens concentration, self-worth, and chances of success. A chunk of carnelian in the house, or a cabochon on a money clip, will guard against poverty. It also helps retain a sense of humor. As a healing stone, carnelian stimulates the appetite and regulates the blood.

This stone makes an excellent battery for storing power and boosting your personal energy. Sometimes you can find it carved into a small egg, sphere, or worry stone—all ideal for this purpose—but a plain tumbled lump will also work. To access the stored power, say:

Spark of the day / Flame of the Sun / Power of light
By this I pray / My will be done: / Lend me your might.

—Elizabeth Barrette

---

17 Saturday
2nd ♑
Color: Brown

---

18 Sunday
2nd ♑
☽ v/c 2:26 pm
Color: Orange

August

19 Monday
2nd ♑
☽ enters ♒ 12:07 am
Color: Lavender

An Elephant totem teaches wisdom, memory, and patience

☺ Tuesday
2nd ♒
☽ v/c 9:45 pm
Full Moon 9:45 pm
Color: Black

Corn Moon

21 Wednesday
3rd ♒
☽ enters ♓ 12:43 am
Color: Yellow

22 Thursday
3rd ♓
☉ enters ♍ 7:02 pm
☽ v/c 9:38 pm
Color: Crimson

Sun enters Virgo

23 Friday
3rd ♓
☽ enters ♈ 3:13 am
☿ enters ♍ 6:36 pm
Color: Rose

Set in Eastern Daylight Time (EDT)

Corn Moon

The word *corn* once referred to any type of grain. Since this is when harvest season begins, this ritual is one of giving thanks. Surround a single white candle with whatever seasonal items you can gather—flowers, herbs, and even fruits and vegetables. See if you can find some sunflowers or marigold for decoration as well. Harvest is a gathering time and in our personal lives we go through cycles as well, like the seasons of planting, growing, and reaping. At this time, reward yourself for your hard work and accomplishments; reflect back on the goal you set in February. Perhaps make plans for a future harvest—prepare the land, metaphorically speaking. Give thanks for the harvest; ask for courage.

Thanks for harvest, blessed yield, / Fruits and grain from the field.
I have gained, I have learned, / I've invested, I have earned.
I have given and received, / In hard times, I believed.
I give thanks and I ask / To be equal to the task.
Seasons end and start anew / Keep me strong, follow through.

—Ember Grant

---

24 Saturday

3rd ♈
Color: Gray

---

25 Sunday

3rd ♈
☽ v/c 6:02 am
☽ enters ♉ 9:13 am
Color: Amber

Tin relates to money and luck;
it is often used in prosperity talismans

---

26 Monday
3rd ♉
Color: Gray

27 Tuesday
3rd ♉
☽ v/c 6:58 pm
☽ enters ♊ 7:08 pm
♂ enters ♌ 10:05 pm
Color: White

Oranges are associated with friendship,
hence the tradition of giving clove-decorated oranges

○ Wednesday
3rd ♊
4th quarter 5:35 am
♀ enters ♍ 6:20 am
Color: Brown

29 Thursday
4th ♊
☽ v/c 12:44 am
Color: Purple

30 Friday
4th ♊
☽ enters ♋ 7:33 am
Color: Coral

Damselflies signify speed, grace, and the element of air

31 Saturday

4th ♋
☽ v/c 8:06 pm
Color: Blue

A ring around the moon predicts rain within three days

1 Sunday

4th ♋
☽ enters ♌ 8:01 pm
Color: Yellow

September

2 Monday
4th ♌
Color: Silver

Labor Day
Celtic Tree Month of Vine begins

3 Tuesday
4th ♌
☽ v/c 1:52 pm
Color: Scarlet

4 Wednesday
4th ♌
☽ enters ♍ 6:43 am
Color: Topaz

Dragon's blood incense boosts magical power

☽ Thursday
4th ♍
New Moon 7:36 am
Color: Crimson

Rosh Hashanah

6 Friday
1st ♍
☽ v/c 6:10 am
☽ enters ♎ 3:12 pm
Color: Coral

Set in Eastern Daylight Time (EDT)

Autumn Mash and Pulled Pork

1 3–4 lb pork shoulder
Dry rub: 1 tsp. each brown sugar,
    salt, black pepper, cumin, paprika,
    and dry ginger
1 bottle beer (I like apricot ale)
8 oz. apple cider
4–6 cloves garlic, peeled
2 onions, quartered
Your favorite barbecue sauce
Picnic buns

Prepare the pulled pork: Pat dry rub
into all sides; set aside for 30 minutes.
Then sear the roast quickly on all sides, using a hot skillet with a little oil.

    Pour the beer and cider into a Dutch oven. Add the roast, fat side up.
Put the garlic and onions around the roast. Cover and roast at 300 degrees
F for about 4 hours. The finished pork should be meltingly tender.

    Pull the pork into soft shreds and pieces. Toss with barbecue sauce to
"wet" thoroughly and serve on warm buns with the mash alongside.

    A great pairing for pulled pork is a sun-gold mash of butternut squash,
potato, and tart-sweet apple—just cube and boil for about 12 minutes in
lightly salted water, drain, mash, and add butter, yogurt, and salt and pepper.

—Susan Pesznecker

---

7 Saturday

1st ♎︎
Color: Black

Amaethon is the
Welsh god of agriculture,
empowered with Earth magic

---

8 Sunday

1st ♎︎
☽ v/c 4:46 pm
☽ enters ♏︎ 9:44 pm
Color: Gold

The holly tree is sacred, and its parts may be used for consecration

---

September

9 Monday

1st ♏

☿ enters ♎ 3:07 am

Color: White

10 Tuesday

1st ♏

⚳ enters ♍ 1:08 am

☽ v/c 5:21 am

Color: Red

Marlin sygnifies agility in maneuvering through life

11 Wednesday

1st ♏

♀ enters ♏ 2:16 am

☽ enters ♐ 2:36 am

⚴ enters ♌ 9:52 am

Color: Yellow

Bes in as African goddess
of pregnancy and childbirth;
she protects new mothers and babies

☽ Thursday

1st ♐

☽ v/c 1:08 pm

2nd quarter 1:08 pm

Color: Green

13 Friday

2nd ♐

☽ enters ♑ 5:56 am

Color: Rose

A length of cotton cord can temporarily store
magic by knotting and then unknotting the cord

Set in Eastern Daylight Time (EDT)

Mabon

The wheel of the year inexorably continues to turn toward darkness. Dusk starts to come a little faster now, and the air is a bit fresher and cooler each morning. Take note of the changing seasons and the leaves as they begin their colorful display. This is the season of Dionysus, lord of the vine. The grape harvest is in, and wines are being produced everywhere. This autumn, go to some local wineries, enjoy the local vineyards, and support your local vintners. Take a  few moments to slow down, relax, and celebrate this enchanted time of the harvest. You can even make this into a family event. Pack a picnic lunch, bring a bottle of fancy grape juice for the kids. The adults can share a bottle of wine and everyone can raise a glass in toast to Dionysus and the harvest!

We thank you for your magick Dionysus lord of the vine,
With much joy and reverence we celebrate the harvest time.
All around us, autumn colors are painted upon the leaves,
May we know the blessings of comfort, bliss, and prosperity.

—Ellen Dugan

14 Saturday

2nd ♑
☽ v/c 7:17 pm
Color: Gray

Yom Kippur

15 Sunday

2nd ♑
☽ enters ♒ 8:05 am
Color: Orange

Dark-green deals with agriculture and Earth magic

September

16 Monday
2nd ♒
☽ v/c 4:19 am
Color: Lavender

To learn about poise and alertness,
study the animal power of Deer

17 Tuesday
2nd ♒
☽ enters ♓ 9:58 am
Color: White

18 Wednesday
2nd ♓
Color: Brown

Sukkot begins

☺ Thursday
2nd ♓
☽ v/c 7:13 am
Full Moon 7:13 am
☽ enters ♈ 12:58 pm
Color: Purple

Harvest Moon

20 Friday
3rd ♈
♇ D 11:29 am
☽ v/c 9:25 pm
Color: Pink

Harvest Moon

Decorate your altar with apples, sheaves of wheat, and white mums; for fragrance, use bergamot, copal, or gardenia. For the Harvest Moon, celebrate with a Moon Goddess Ritual to honor the Maiden, Mother, and Crone—this represents change: the cycles of life and seasons. With this ritual we honor the change of seasons and the Moon. You may dedicate this ritual to a specific Moon Goddess if you'd like.

Maiden, Mother, and Crone, all Goddesses of the Moon,
tonight I honor You. You mirror the cycles of life.
Your way is subtle, changing, and from this we gain Your wisdom.
You mirror the sun. When you shine, You help us see,
give us light in darkness, so we can look into the light
with unguarded eyes. And when you are hidden, you remind us
the darkness is also beautiful and filled with mystery.
Tonight I seek Your blessing, Moon Goddesses, three faces in one.

—Ember Grant

21 Saturday

3rd ♈
☽ enters ♉ 6:33 pm
Color: Brown

UN International Day of Peace

22 Sunday

3rd ♉
☉ enters ♎ 4:44 pm
Color: Amber

Mabon/Fall Equinox
Sun enters Libra

September

23 Monday

3rd ♉
☽ v/c 3:13 am
Color: Ivory

Aluminum represents the planet Mercury and communication

24 Tuesday

3rd ♉
☿ D 3:17 am
☽ enters ♊ 3:34 am
Color: Gray

Fireflies show enlightenment and guidance

25 Wednesday

3rd ♊
Color: White

Sukkot ends

◑ Thursday

3rd ♊
☽ v/c 7:21 am
☽ enters ♋ 3:24 pm
4th quarter 11:55 pm
Color: Turquoise

27 Friday

4th ♋
Color: Purple

*A pecan in your pocket boosts
your chances in a job interview*

Set in Eastern Daylight Time (EDT)

Sardonyx

Sardonyx has a cryptocrystalline structure appearing in large masses. Color is reddish-brown banded with black or white. Artisans use it in cameo and bas-relief, one layer as background and a contrasting layer as foreground figures. Ruled by Mars, sardonyx relates to the sign of Capricorn, the root chakra, and the element of fire.

It promotes justice, a good choice for anyone in law enforcement. In ritual work, sardonyx amplifies bonfire or candle magic. Emotionally, it fosters loyalty and stability; it is believed to bring a new marriage or support an existing one. As a healing stone, it relieves back pain and menstrual cramps.

Sardonyx creates a sense of self and security. It grants courage when people feel like they don't fit in. Ideally, use a sardonyx cameo of something sturdy, such as a tree or a bull; but a plain piece of jewelry or tumbled stone will do. Attune it with these words (repeat as needed when under stress):

Blood as deep as bone / Roots as strong as stone
Always stay my own / Never feel alone.

—Elizabeth Barrette

---

28 Saturday
4th ♋
Color: Indigo

Spilling pepper predicts an argument

---

29 Sunday
4th ♋
☽ v/c 3:30 am
☽ enters ♌ 3:57 am
☿ enters ♏ 7:38 am
Color: Yellow

September/October

30 Monday
4th ♌
Color: Gray

Celtic Tree Month of Ivy begins

1 Tuesday
4th ♌
☽ v/c 12:48 am
☽ enters ♍ 2:52 pm
Color: White

2 Wednesday
4th ♍
Color: Yellow

Burn oakmoss to attract wealth

3 Thursday
4th ♍
☽ v/c 2:57 pm
☽ enters ♎ 10:59 pm
Color: Turquoise

Friday
4th ♎
New Moon 8:35 pm
Color: Coral

Ganesha is the Hindu god of knowledge,
empowered to remove obstacles

Set in Eastern Daylight Time (EDT)

5 Saturday

1st ♎
☽ v/c 6:28 pm
Color: Blue

*The almond tree symbolizes innocence
and fruitfulness; good for young lovers*

6 Sunday

1st ♎
☽ enters ♏ 4:33 am
Color: Gold

October

7 Monday

1st ♏
♀ enters ♐ 1:54 pm
Color: White

Orca symbolizes personal freedom and empowerment

8 Tuesday

1st ♏
☽ v/c 12:54 am
☽ enters ♐ 8:21 am
Color: Red

Anahita is a Zoroastrian goddess of the moon, fertility, and water

9 Wednesday

1st ♐
Color: Brown

10 Thursday

1st ♐
☽ v/c 6:10 am
☽ enters ♑ 11:17 am
Color: Purple

A mirror may be enchanted to deflect
negative energy, thus protecting the bearer

◑ Friday

1st ♑
2nd quarter 7:02 pm
☽ v/c 8:04 pm
Color: Rose

Tourmaline

Tourmaline forms hexagonal crystals that are either transparent, translucent, or opaque. It comes in all colors, often bicolored, such as watermelon tourmaline (pinkish red inside, green outside). Some are pleochroic, changing color.

Legendarily, tourmaline got its colors traveling on a rainbow, so it does weather magic. It relates to air. It strengthens the body and spirit. For healing, it supports nervous, circulatory, and lymphatic systems. Tourmaline talismans aid creativity among writers and artisans.

A chakra pendant supports your energy system, especially one with all tourmalines. Before wearing over your heart chakra, attune with this charm:

Black for the Earth below, / Red for the root,
Orange for the sacral, / Yellow for the solar plexus,
Green for the heart, / Blue for the throat,
Indigo for the third eye, / Violet for the crown,
Clear for the Heavens above— / Support me with your love.

—Elizabeth Barrette

---

12 Saturday

2nd ♑
☽ enters ♒ 2:00 pm
Color: Black

---

13 Sunday

2nd ♒
Color: Yellow

Royal blue increases happiness and loyalty

October

14 Monday
2nd ♒︎
☽ v/c 4:28 pm
☽ enters ♓︎ 5:06 pm
Color: Gray

Columbus Day (observed)

15 Tuesday

2nd ♓︎
♂ enters ♍︎ 7:05 am
Color: Black

16 Wednesday

2nd ♓︎
☽ v/c 3:15 am
☽ enters ♈︎ 9:18 pm
Color: White

Cougar as a totem presents strength with grace

17 Thursday
2nd ♈︎
Color: Crimson

☺ Friday
2nd ♈︎
☽ v/c 7:38 pm
Full Moon 7:38 pm
Color: Pink

Blood Moon
Lunar eclipse 7:50 pm, 25° ♈︎ 51'

Set in Eastern Daylight Time (EDT)

Blood Moon

This time of year, our ancestors would have been busy preparing for the long winter ahead—and naturally, contemplating death and our very existence. Ponder these things too, as you honor the blood that sustains human life. For your ritual, light a red candle in a jar and burn dragon's blood or patchouli incense. Pour a goblet of pomegranate juice to use as your ritual beverage, symbolizing lifeblood: the blood of animals from the hunt and livestock, and the blood in your veins.

In the sacred night the blood is spilled
By the hunt and harvest life fulfilled
Blessed be the animals and grains
Blessed be the earth and sun and rain.

In the sacred night a candle burns,
Every night and day the wheel turns,
Sun and moon trade places in the sky,
Guiding us as every year goes by.
                                    —Ember Grant

---

19 Saturday

3rd ♈
☽ enters ♉ 3:27 am
Color: Brown

Lead corresponds to the planet Saturn and bindings

---

20 Sunday

3rd ♉
☽ v/c 5:02 pm
Color: Orange

October

21 Monday

3rd ♉
☿ ℞ 6:29 am
☽ enters ♊ 12:14 pm
Color: Lavender

For courage, carry sprigs of yarrow and thyme

22 Tuesday

3rd ♊
☽ v/c 8:35 pm
Color: White

23 Wednesday

3rd ♊
☉ enters ♏ 2:10 am
☽ enters ♋ 11:36 pm
Color: Topaz

Sun enters Scorpio

24 Thursday

3rd ♋
Color: Green

Grasshopper represents a leap of faith

25 Friday

3rd ♋
☽ v/c 4:31 pm
Color: Purple

Set in Eastern Daylight Time (EDT)

Hungry Horde Magick Bean Sandwich

1 piece sturdy bread (homemade
   or artisan)
*Leftover baked beans,
   gently warmed
Thin slices of sweet onion
Thick slices of ripe tomato
Sliced sharp cheddar cheese
2–3 slices bacon, uncooked

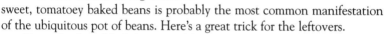

At Samhain, tasty and nutritious bean
dishes are a quick, economical way to
feed a sabbat crowd. A big crock of
sweet, tomatoey baked beans is probably the most common manifestation
of the ubiquitous pot of beans. Here's a great trick for the leftovers.

Toast the bread lightly. Spread beans on the toasted bread. Lay the
onions and tomato over the beans and top with cheese slices. Arrange
bacon pieces over the bread, completely covering it.

Place the sandwich on a foil-lined baking sheet. Broil for 5 to 6 minutes or until the bacon cooks. Serve with knife and fork.

*I start with a giant can of pre-made baked beans and doctor them up
with ketchup, yellow mustard, sautéed onions, cooked bacon pieces, and
brown sugar (and sometimes a can of drained black beans).

—Susan Pesznecker

☽ Saturday

3rd ♋
☽ enters ♌ 12:12 pm
4th quarter 7:40 pm
Color: Gray

A swan feather sewn into a lover's pillow encourages fidelity

---

27 Sunday

4th ♌
Color: Amber

---

28 Monday

4th ♌
☽ v/c 8:26 am
☽ enters ♍ 11:45 pm
Color: White

Celtic Tree Month of Reed begins

29 Tuesday

4th ♍
Color: Scarlet

30 Wednesday

4th ♍
☽ v/c 10:48 pm
Color: Yellow

31 Thursday

4th ♍
☽ enters ♎ 8:22 am
Color: Purple

Samhain/Halloween

1 Friday

4th ♎
Color: White

All Saints' Day

Set in Eastern Daylight Time (EDT)

Samhain

Halloween decorations are rife with symbols of the Crone goddess, and these trendy dark and gothic trappings are great for working transformative magick with her. Consider those ebony and amethyst candleholders, sparkling black tapers, candles shaped like skulls, silk but real-looking ravens and crows. This Samhain, why not go all out with a Crone altar dedicated to the Greek goddess Hecate? Hecate is a Triple Goddess and also a patron of Witches, sorcerers, and magicians. Tonight the veil between worlds is at its thinnest. Spirits walk, the Old Ones are out among us, and magick is ripe. Call upon Hecate for the wisdom to work with these types of energies.

Samhain has come, the veil between the worlds is thin,
Chilly winds now blow, and the fallen leaves do spin.
With this Crone altar, I celebrate your special time,
This Samhain spell is now cast with the sound of a rhyme.
Hecate, light my path on this magickal night,
Grant me your courage and grace, wisdom, and insight.

—Ellen Dugan

2 Saturday

4th ♎
☽ v/c 8:47 am
☽ enters ♏ 1:35 pm
Color: Blue

Vetivert incense encourages feelings of love and peace

☽ Sunday

4th ♏
New Moon 7:50 am
♀ enters ♎ 9:15 am
☽ v/c 11:23 pm
Color: Yellow

Solar eclipse 7:46 am, 11° ♏ 16'
Daylight Saving Time ends at 2 am

November

4 Monday

1st ♏
☽ enters ♐ 3:14 pm
Color: Silver

5 Tuesday

1st ♐
♀ enters ♑ 3:43 am
☽ v/c 11:48 am
Color: Black

Islamic New Year
Election Day (general)

6 Wednesday

1st ♐
☽ enters ♑ 4:44 pm
Color: Brown

7 Thursday

1st ♑
♃ ℞ 12:03 am
Color: Green

Samhain crossquarter day
(Sun reaches 15° Scorpio)

8 Friday

1st ♑
☽ v/c 2:39 am
☽ enters ♒ 6:30 pm
Color: Coral

Set in Eastern Daylight Time (EDT)

9 Saturday

1st ♒

♀ enters ♍ 7:17 pm

Color: Gray

Agunua is a snake god from the Solomon Islands,
to whom people give the first coconut harvested from each tree

☐ Sunday

1st ♒

☽ v/c 12:57 am

2nd quarter 12:57 am

☿ D 4:12 pm

☽ enters ♓ 9:36 pm

Color: Gold

The peach tree symbolizes marriage and domestic happiness

November

11 Monday

2nd ♓
Color: White

Veterans Day

12 Tuesday

2nd ♓
☽ v/c 9:34 am
Color: Red

13 Wednesday
2nd ♓
☽ enters ♈ 2:39 am
♆ D 1:42 pm
Color: Yellow

Salmon embodies the knowledge
of when to wait and when to leap forward

14 Thursday
2nd ♈
☽ v/c 3:57 pm
Color: Purple

15 Friday

2nd ♈
⚷ enters ♎ 8:45 am
☽ enters ♉ 9:49 am
Color: Rose

Yondung Halmoni is a Korean wind goddess;
people honor her with rituals and feed her rice cakes

Set in Eastern Standard Time (EST)

Hunter's Moon

For the November Full Moon celebration, decorate your altar with white pumpkins and gourds, and a branch of cedar. This Moon is also often called the Snow Moon. Think of yourself on the hunt as a spiritual quest and use this ritual as an introspection or meditation—visualize yourself walking through snowy woods in the moonlight. Light white candles and see yourself carrying one of these candles through the woods, like a miniature moon glowing inside a lantern. Recite the chant and imagine yourself on a journey for enlightenment.

Seeking, questing, search within—
Moonlight watch as I begin.
Seeking, questing, search without—
Moonlight shine upon my doubt.
Show me what I need to know,
Hunter's Moon I feel your glow.

—Ember Grant

---

16 Saturday

2nd ♉
Color: Black

☺ Sunday

2nd ♉
☽ v/c 10:16 am
Full Moon 10:16 am
☽ enters ♊ 7:07 pm
Color: Amber

Mourning Moon

November

18 Monday

3rd ♊
Color: Gray

Light-blue promotes peace and tranquility

19 Tuesday

3rd ♊
☿ D 8:07 am
☽ v/c 10:59 am
Color: Scarlet

*A whistle made of alder can
summon and influence the four winds*

20 Wednesday

3rd ♊
☽ enters ♋ 6:23 am
Color: White

21 Thursday

3rd ♋
☉ enters ♐ 10:48 pm
Color: Turquoise

Sun enters Sagittarius

22 Friday

3rd ♋
☽ v/c 2:11 am
☽ enters ♌ 6:56 pm
Color: Pink

Set in Eastern Standard Time (EST)

Citrine

Citrine forms hexagonal crystals, often clusters or geodes. Color is pale yellow, orange, or brown. Citrine is the November birthstone and the planetary stone for Virgo. As a marriage token, it is the customary jewel for both the 13th and the 17th wedding anniversaries.

Magically, citrine emits a warm positive energy that repels evil and promotes optimism. It opens the mind to intuition and good instincts. It helps to weather change. It fosters a sense of security. A citrine necklace helps public speakers, enhancing the voice and charisma. It aids quick thinking and decision-making skills. For healing, it boosts the body's natural energy.

Citrine promotes wealth and success for business or home finances. Place a large crystal point in or near the cash register. Or set a faceted gem in a money clip, checkbook cover, etc. Attune it with this chant:

Crystal of light, / Power of right.
Color of gold, / Money to hold.
Color of sun, / Success be won.

—Elizabeth Barrette

23 Saturday
3rd ♌
Color: Brown

Chrome relates to the sign of Gemini and the power of duality

24 Sunday
3rd ♌
☽ v/c 3:59 am
Color: Orange

Solitary people may benefit from working with
Bobcat, exploring ways to be alone yet not lonely

November/December

○ Monday

3rd ♌
☽ enters ♍ 7:11 am
4th quarter 2:28 pm
Color: Lavender

Celtic Tree Month of Elder begins

26 Tuesday

4th ♍
Color: White

Witch hazel and rosemary enhance beauty

27 Wednesday

4th ♍
☽ v/c 6:44 am
☽ enters ♎ 5:00 pm
Color: Topaz

28 Thursday

4th ♎
Color: Crimson

Thanksgiving Day
Hanukkah begins

29 Friday

4th ♎
☽ v/c 6:13 am
☽ enters ♏ 11:03 pm
Color: Purple

Katydids symbolize intuition and sensitivity

Set in Eastern Standard Time (EST)

30 Saturday

4th ♏

Color: Indigo

A string of chilies and lemons will ward off the evil eye

1 Sunday

4th ♏

☽ v/c 8:34 pm

Color: Amber

December

☽ Monday
4th ♏

☽ enters ♐ 1:31 am
New Moon 7:22 pm
Color: Ivory

Ylang-ylang incense promotes harmony and feminine energy

3 Tuesday
1st ♐
☽ v/c 10:45 pm
Color: Gray

Multultu is an Australian creator god, taking the form of a kangaroo

4 Wednesday
1st ♐
☽ enters ♑ 1:49 am
☿ enters ♐ 9:42 pm
Color: Yellow

5 Thursday
1st ♑
Color: Purple

Hanukkah ends

6 Friday
1st ♑
☽ v/c 12:31 am
☽ enters ♒ 1:53 am
Color: Pink

Set in Eastern Standard Time (EST)

Festive Cranberry Salad

2 cups whole raw cranberries,
  washed and patted dry
1 cup sugar
20 oz. crushed pineapple in its
  own juice, well drained
1 cup heavy whipping cream (try
  to avoid ultra-pasteurized varieties)
1 bag miniature marshmallows

When I was little, I always called this
"pink salad," and the name has stuck
in our family. But this recipe is simple,
inexpensive, beautiful, tasty, and festive-looking to boot—much more
than just "pink" and a lovely addition to your celebratory table.

6 to 8 hours (or up to one day) before serving: Use a food processor to
finely chop the raw cranberries. Combine with sugar in a large bowl and
allow to sit for 2 hours—this draws out the juice. After the cranberries have
finished sitting, add the drained pineapple and stir well.

Whip the cream. Add it to the bowl along with 1 cup miniature marshmallows. Fold the cream and marshmallows gently into the cranberries and
pineapple, blending without deflating the cream. Taste with a clean spoon;
add additional marshmallows if desired. Chill until serving.

—Susan Pesznecker

7 Saturday

1st ≈
☽ v/c 7:11 am
♂ enters ♎ 3:41 pm
Color: Blue

8 Sunday

1st ≈
☽ enters ♓ 3:34 am
Color: Yellow

The coconut tree represents femininity and good milk flow

December

◐ Monday

1st ♓
2nd quarter 10:12 am
Color: Gray

10 Tuesday

2nd ♓
☽ v/c 1:41 am
☽ enters ♈ 8:06 am
Color: White

Seahorse symbolizes fatherhood
and the nurturing aspect of masculinity

11 Wednesday

2nd ♈
Color: Brown

Ekadzati is a Tibetan
goddess of wisdom,
portrayed with a single eye

12 Thursday

2nd ♈
☽ v/c 10:37 am
☽ enters ♉ 3:40 pm
Color: Crimson

13 Friday

2nd ♉
Color: Rose

A forked hazel stick can divine truth or falsehood

Set in Eastern Standard Time (EST)

Yule

The Winter Solstice season is all about light and faith. Faith that the Sun and warmth will return to the land, and hope in humanity. In this season of celebration and light, consider the Greek god of the Sun, Apollo, a solar deity associated with music, poetry, illumination, knowledge, and prophecy. Apollo challenges you with the message inscribed at his temple in Delphi: "Know thyself." Be true to yourself. Dare to follow your own path and to challenge yourself to learn and to grow.

Then use your will and create a positive change. Accomplish your personal and magickal goals, not only for yourself but for the loved ones in your life.

Apollo, ancient god of the Sun now hear my call,
Bring illumination whether rain or snowflakes fall.
On this the darkest and longest of winter's bleak nights,
I celebrate the return of the Sun's strength and light.
May my own truth shine free for all to see,
And as I will it, then so must it be.

—Ellen Dugan

14 Saturday

2nd ♉
☽ v/c 9:54 pm
Color: Black

Lavender is the color of righteousness and guiding spirits

15 Sunday

2nd ♉
☽ enters ♊ 1:40 am
Color: Gold

December

16 Monday
2nd ♊
Color: White

Tuesday
2nd ♊
☽ v/c 4:28 am
Full Moon 4:28 am
♅ D 12:40 pm
☽ enters ♋ 1:17 pm
Color: Black

Long Nights Moon

18 Wednesday
3rd ♋
Color: Topaz

Antelope as a totem teaches about opportunities and instincts

19 Thursday
3rd ♋
☽ v/c 11:37 pm
Color: Green

20 Friday
3rd ♋
☽ enters ♌ 1:48 am
Color: Coral

Nickel corresponds to the sign
of Virgo and the quality of precision

Set in Eastern Standard Time (EST)

Long Nights Moon

Just as the Sun and Moon were honored at the time of the Strong Sun Moon for the strength of light, so once again we honor them during the month when nights dominate. We have less sunlight now than any other time. To celebrate the light, gather as many candles as you possibly can and arrange them in a circle. Use white or silver if you have them, as well as gold. Decorate your altar with celestial symbols and shapes: suns, moons, and stars.

Sister Moon, tempered light,
Bringing Sun into the night.
Darkness long, darkness deep
Moonlight strong, vigil keep.
Light of stars, light of life
Cut the dark like a knife.
Sister Moon, tempered light,
Bringing Sun into the night.
—Ember Grant

---

21 Saturday

3rd ♌
☉ enters ♑ 12:11 pm
♀ ℞ 4:53 pm
Color: Brown

Yule/Winter Solstice
Sun enters Capricorn

---

22 Sunday

3rd ♌
☽ v/c 8:25 am
☽ enters ♍ 2:19 pm
Color: Orange

Celtic Tree Month of Elder ends

Set in Eastern Standard Time (EST)   129

December

23 Monday
3rd ♍
Color: Silver

Between (Celtic Tree Month)

24 Tuesday
3rd ♍
☿ enters ♑ 5:12 am
☽ v/c 10:55 pm
Color: Red

Christmas Eve
Celtic Tree Month of Birch begins

○ Wednesday
3rd ♍
☽ enters ♎ 1:17 am
4th quarter 8:48 am
Color: White

Christmas Day

26 Thursday
4th ♎
Color: Purple

Kwanzaa begins

27 Friday
4th ♎
☽ v/c 6:00 am
☽ enters ♏ 8:58 am
Color: Pink

Set in Eastern Standard Time (EST)

Onyx

Onyx has a trigonal crystal structure with a vitreous luster, usually appearing in masses. The color is black, sometimes banded with white. It is often used for carving statuettes, seals, small jars, etc. As jewelry, it may be faceted or cabochon in form. Onyx is the traditional December birthstone, the talismanic stone for Capricorn, and the Star Sign stone for Leo. Onyx relates to the element of earth.

Magically, onyx absorbs evil and eliminates negative thoughts. It fosters a spiritual connection and sharpens the wits. As a healing stone, it strengthens the heart and kidneys. It also reduces stress, improves neurological problems, and promotes restful sleep. Onyx can relieve apathy and nurture regrowth. It alleviates unwanted lust. An excellent grounding stone, onyx helps flighty people to concentrate and stay focused. Onyx helps break bad habits. A worry stone or tumbled stone is ideal, but a ring or pendant also works. Charge it with these words:

Bad habit, bane and bone, / Go now into this stone!
Let none be as before. / Go! Trouble me no more.

—Elizabeth Barrette

---

28 Saturday
4th ♏
Color: Gray

29 Sunday
4th ♏
☽ v/c 8:54 am
☽ enters ♐ 12:37 pm
Color: Amber

For spells to relieve anxiety, use valerian and skullcap

December/January

30 Monday

4th ♐
☽ v/c 6:36 am
Color: Ivory

Rain on a wedding day predict
wealth and success for the coupl

31 Tuesday

4th ♐
☽ enters ♑ 1:01 pm
Color: Black

New Year's Eve

☽ Wednesday

4th ♑
⚹ enters ♓ 2:14 am
New Moon 6:14 am
Color: Yellow

New Year's Da
Kwanzaa end

2 Thursday

1st ♑
☽ v/c 6:12 am
☽ enters ♒ 12:03 pm
Color: Crimson

3 Friday

1st ♒
☽ v/c 9:43 am
Color: Pink

Set in Eastern Standard Time (EST)

Calcite

Calcite has a hexagonal crystal system but can form many different shapes. Rhombohedral, prismatic, and needle-like crystals occur; the stone can also form large solid masses. It relates to Venus, the Moon, and the astrological sign Cancer. Calcite's mystical properties depend on its color. Clear corresponds with air, inspiring a lightness of being. White calcite connects with the Moon, feminine energy, and water. Pink grounds and centers,

fostering self-love and the ability to love others. Red corresponds to fire and opens the heart chakra. Orange generates joy and energy. Golden relates to solar energy and earth and fire; a good healing stone, it relieves depression. Green connects to earth, bringing prosperity and good luck. Blue corresponds to water; it promotes peace, reconciliation, and sleep.

Calcite is a very soft stone. It is often carved into geometric shapes such as spheres, cubes, and pyramids rather than used for jewelry. You can also find it in crystal form or as a large rough chunk. It transmits its energy well by skin contact, so this makes an excellent large-size worry stone or paperweight. Simply hold it in your hand while meditating on your purpose.

—Elizabeth Barrette

4 Saturday

1st ♒
☽ enters ♓ 11:58 am
Color: Blue

5 Sunday

1st ♓
Color: Gold

Ladybugs stand for persistence
and the ability to outlast challenging times

About the Authors

ELIZABETH BARRETTE was the managing editor of *PanGaia* and has been involved with the Pagan community for twenty years, actively networking via coffeehouse meetings and open sabbats. Her other writings include speculativ... fiction and gender studies. Her 2005 poem "The Poltergeist of Polaris" earne... a nomination for the Rhysling Award. She lives in central Illinois and enjo... herbal landscaping and gardening for wildlife.

DALLAS JENNIFER COBB lives a magical life, manifesting meaningful and fle... ible work, satisfying relationships, and abundant gardens. She enjoys a balanc... of time and money, which support her deepest desires: a loving family, time in nature, self expression, and a healthy home. She lives in paradise, in a water-front village in rural Ontario. Contact her at jennifer.cobb@live.com.

RAVEN DIGITALIS is the author of *Empathy, Planetary Spells & Rituals, Shadow Magick Compendium*, and *Goth Craft*. He is a Neopagan Priest and cofounder of the "Eastern Hellenistic" magickal system and training coven Opus Aima Obscuræ. He is also trained in Georgian Witchcraft and Buddhist philosophy. Raven holds a degree in anthropology from the University of Montana and is also an animal rights activist, black-and-white photographic artist, and tarot reader. A regular contributor to *Dragon's Blood* and *The Ninth Gate* magazines, he has also been featured on MTV News and CBS PsychicRadio. For more, visit www.ravendigitalis .com, www.myspace.com/oakraven, or www.facebook.com/ravendigitalisauthor.

ELLEN DUGAN, the "Garden Witch," is a psychic-clairvoyant and a practicing Witch of twenty years. Ellen is a master gardener who teaches flower folklore and gardening at a community college and is the author of several Llewellyn